Alexander Armstrong

In a Mule Litter to the Tomb of Confucius

Alexander Armstrong

In a Mule Litter to the Tomb of Confucius

ISBN/EAN: 9783743422384

Manufactured in Europe, USA, Canada, Australia, Japa

Cover: Foto ©ninafisch / pixelio.de

Manufactured and distributed by brebook publishing software (www.brebook.com)

Alexander Armstrong

In a Mule Litter to the Tomb of Confucius

IN A MULE LITTER

TO THE

TOMB OF CONFUCIUS

BY

ALEX. ARMSTRONG, F.R.G.S.

London
JAMES NISBET & CO.
21 BERNERS STREET
1896

Printed by BALLANTYNE, HANSON & CO.
At the Ballantyne Press

CONTENTS

CHAPTER I

PAGE

Warnings—Roads (?)—Means of travel—Preparation—The start—Dogs—Shentzŭ travelling—Our first night—A Chinese inn 1–9

CHAPTER II

Grumbles—The man with the cleaver—Many visitors—Shentzŭ and theories break down — Lai-yang — An amazing structure—Three courses at dinner—Carts and combinations—Pateo curses—A bright companion—Swine herds—Holywater Pool—The temple of a thousand idols 10–19

CHAPTER III

A stranger and pilgrim—Gold mines—Pea-nuts—An affable landlord—Difficult dialect—Some boisterous neighbours—Mr. Bow-without-the-String—Evening worship—A pleasant surprise—American Presbyterian Mission, Wei-hsien—Early days—A Chinese preacher . . 20–31

CONTENTS

CHAPTER IV

PAGE

The barrowman and assistant—Pungent straw-smoke, a shrill-voiced landlady, and a yelping cur—The ferrymen and the field-glass — Wayside watch-houses— English Baptist Mission, Ch'ing-chou-fu — Euclid, Book III.—Ch'ing-chou antiquities—A Manchu city —Christmas—A Buddhist hell 32-41

CHAPTER V

A lady companion—Dr. W——'s barrow—The Princes' Pyramids—Mulberry, red date, poplars—Mencius and Niu-shan—Learn young : learn well—" Magnet Hill " —An excited village—Rain and mud—Rested and refreshed at Ts'ou-p'ing—" He searched for a leg for the stool " 42-50

CHAPTER VI

Frost and snow—Chinese at work and play—Another breakdown—Carter and muleteer—New Year's Day —The playful pig of the " Eternally Comfortable "— " Foreign devil "—The city gate—" That rear mule " —Arrival at the capital of the province—Dreams . 51-60

CHAPTER VII

Chi-nan-fu— People — The bitterness of the scholars— Roman Catholic Cathedral—The city's water supply— The city lake—Carvings on the hills—View from the hill—The foreign cemetery—Sunday in Chi-nan— Mission work in the city . . . . , . . 61-70

CONTENTS

CHAPTER VIII
PAGE

Outside the unfriendly city—Hiring a donkey—A donkey ride—Sweet potatoes—Rough roads—A camel cavalcade—Church of England Mission, T'ai-an-fu—The city—The sacred mountain, T'ai-shan—A transformation scene—Complimented by travellers—A bad fix—The classic Ssŭ-ho 71–82

CHAPTER IX

Ch'ü-fou-hsien, the city of Confucius—Confucius no mythical character—The road to the tomb—Chinese slipshodness—Temples and pavilions—Sacred mound—Other great men—General appearance of grounds—Graves, graves, graves 83–91

CHAPTER X

Turn towards home—"That rear mule"—Horse rest place, and "The Bounteous Cavern"—English into Latin, please—A march in the dark—Candles—Snow—"The Bridegroom cometh"—The baggage donkey's spasms—Sawdust and dough—The villainous innkeeper of "The Heavenly Resting Hall"—A warm bed at "The White Pagoda"—Mine host offers opium—Wolves—A trembling guide—A jinricksha and a steam whistle—Dr. Williamson—Telegraph poles . . . 92–105

CHAPTER XI

Ch'ing-chou-fu again—The Christian barrowman—The old evangelist—The Mi-ho boatmen—Have the Chinese any gratitude?—"The Everlasting Peaceful"—Limping—A Chinese Shylock—Wei-hsien plains . . 106–117

CHAPTER XII

Deep snow, bitter cold—The Huai-ho flotilla—"That mule" again—A slippery bridge—A characteristic conversation—A good inn—South-east instead of "East-north"—Soapstone ornaments at Lai-chou-fu—A use for wine—A full market—American Southern Baptist Mission, Huang-hsien 118–130

CHAPTER XIII

A late start—Heavy travelling—Snowed up—Patience—The man who knew the ancients—"Beat with the Whip, and the Rush Flowers fly"—The Noble Middleman 131–141

CHAPTER XIV

Ups and downs—"The Beacon Comfort"—Ku-hsien, the scene of the murder of two missionaries, 1861—The graves of kings 142–147

IN A MULE LITTER
TO
THE TOMB OF CONFUCIUS

CHAPTER I

BEFORE setting out on a journey, the intending traveller is often loaded with warnings and advice by those who have, or are supposed to have, some experience. Let me warn my readers, before they set out, that they must not expect anything thrilling. I had no hair-breadth escapes, nor was I privileged to snatch any one from imminent death. Still, those who accompany me with eyes and ears open in this strange land may see and hear things that will go far to repay them for their trouble.

Let me say first of all, then, that foreigners who have been accustomed with anything like macadamised roads can have little or no idea of the meaning of the word "road" as applied to the highways of Shantung—the Province in China in which this journey was made. Perhaps the most important road in the province is the one which runs from Chefoo to the capital, Chi-nan-fu. Carts can go over its whole length, but the part from Chefoo to Huang-hsien is very rough and rocky. At other parts further west the road is from twenty to sixty feet wide, formed merely by a series of ruts. Again, at other places, where it is impossible to extend itself in breadth, the traffic has worn cuttings into the clayey soil thirty or forty feet deep. Some of the rivers can be crossed at bridges, some by ferry, and at others—well, one has to run the risk of getting a ducking at a ford.

The traveller may ride a donkey, a mule, or a pony; or he may use a barrow, a cart, a sedan chair, a boat, or a shentzŭ. Concerning all of these, except, perhaps, the last named, most readers know something. The shentzŭ belongs more particularly to the north, and might be best described as a large sedan chair having an arched roof, the floor of the chair roomy enough to let a person lie on it; but whereas the chair is carried on men's shoulders, the shafts of the shentzŭ rest on the backs of mules. *Shentzŭ* is the Chinese name for what we would call a mule litter. As this conveyance can go over almost any kind of road, I decided on it, and engaged two mules for the litter, and a donkey for the baggage: the three animals with the shentzŭ and a man cost 1300 cash per day when we travelled, and 700 cash per day when we rested from any cause.

Once I took a short journey without making a definite arrangement with the coolies as to payment before we set out. One such experience is quite enough. The traveller should always make sure before he starts that a clear understanding has been come to between himself and the party he has engaged. Is the litter to travel and to stay just as he orders? If not able to travel on account of the weather, how much per day is to be paid? If delayed by the traveller's own desire, how much per day? Is the muleteer to be paid daily the whole sum agreed upon, or how much in advance? Such questions as these should never be left to be settled on the road: the muleteer has the traveller too much in his hands then for a fair arrangement to be made.

Oh, the talk, the volumes of talk that one has to get through before anything like a reasonable bargain is come to! But at last it is settled, and the day is fixed for the start—you may fix the hour too, but you save yourself trouble by being independent as to hours. Hours! What paltry things are hours to a Chinaman. Days, moons, years, he understands; but hours! Ah!

Now, while the muleteer is making his arrangements for being away from home thirty or forty days, we must not be idle. Books and tracts must be got ready. A little foreign food, too, must be packed into as small space as possible to be taken with us. And what about money for the journey? Ah, that is an important if troublesome item. Fortunately my Chinese teacher has just come in, and as we have often spoken about this journey, and he is delighted at the prospect of becoming a traveller, he is not surprised when I say to him—in Chinese, of course—lit. trans.: "The teacher arrived, good. Invite teacher to buy-sell-silver shop go. May buy one piece shoe silver, good, about fifty ounces. Take to blacksmith. Blacksmith chop into pieces, one, two, three ounce. Weigh carefully, and mark on each piece his weight." (One ounce of silver will buy from 1200 to 1600 cash. The traveller buys cash as he requires it on his journey.)

When the time comes for the start to be made there are a great many chances to one that the muleteer does not put in his appearance till at least a couple of hours later than you had expected. And when he does arrive he protests at the quantity of baggage. "The goods will not fit into the bottom of the shentzŭ;" "They are too heavy;" "We shall never be able to get on;" "If anything goes wrong I must not be blamed," &c. I may state that at this point the silence of a foreigner is much more effective than his speech.

At length everything is ready. Good-byes are

said, and I am off, actually off, accompanied by my teacher and a servant.

We left Chefoo at 2.30 P.M. on Monday, 15th December, and had a pretty rough bit of road immediately after we started. Going up a steep pass, almost due south of Temple Hill, made the mules blow in a most unsatisfactory manner. I was well done-up myself when I got to the top, and was more than pleased to rest a little and look down upon fading Yen-t'ai (the Chinese name for Chefoo), before the hills would shut it from my sight for weeks. Whether it was regret at leaving my home, or what it was, I will not say, but it was not without a pang that I turned my back upon Settlement Hill, and set forward on an altogether untried path.

Every person we met or passed treated me with the most perfect respect. Only the curs of dogs seemed to have banded together to eat me up. In their well-known cowardly way, however, they turned and fled at my first attempt at self-defence. It is one of the remarkable traits of those dogs that they will lie snoozing at the doors of their masters' houses and permit hundreds of ordinary Chinese, if not beggars, to pass them unchallenged; but if a foreigner comes near them, instantly they are up, all bristles. Again and again in past years I have had this experience, even when dressed exactly as the Chinese. They seem, indeed, to scent the enemy from afar. The Chinese themselves think that we foreigners smell horribly. A washer-woman at the Gank'ing Training Home gave up her work there and a good wage, as she could not continue to do the washing, "The clothes smelt so strongly of mutton," she said. And yet it must be some other thing than the sense of smell that guides the dogs; for they will noisily attack every beggar, and will only cease barking and growling when they have got the intruder off their masters' premises.

After walking twenty-five *li*—a li is about one-third of an English mile—I essayed to get up into my shentzŭ. But it was no easy matter. A mule is a mule anywhere, but I think those mules were more mulish than most mules. When wanted to stand, of course that was the very time when they seemed bent on finishing their journey—and mine—as soon as possible. As long as they kept moving I could not get into my seat. Now they are steady, and the muleteer bends his leg so that I can use his knee as a step by which to get up. Alas! one of the long ears is turned towards us, and our plan is spoiled. I could easily get seated, but I must not lean much on the one side or on the other; if I do, the whole arrangement would topple off the backs of the mules. At length, however, I get to my seat, and we move along merrily. The baggage donkey was not so much burdened but that the teacher could mount on the top of the goods, and make himself comfortable. There he sat, with his hat just a little bit to the side, with all the air of a schoolboy off for a holiday. As long as the weather kept good my teacher was much more comfortable than I was. He could see about him nicely; I could not. The only view that I had was right before, as the sides and back of the shentzŭ had no windows. Then, again, he was, so to speak, at the mercy of one donkey, while I was left to the clemency of two cross-purposed mules and a muleteer.

Dear reader, I speak feelingly, have you ever seen a bottle in the act of being washed out? If you have, just fancy what it would be like for you to be not only the bottle but the contents. From stopper to bottom the contents are dashed, up and down, down and up: the mules step nicely together. Then the mules get out of step and the process is changed; the contents of the bottle are swilled from side to side. Then the long-ears step together again, and the contents are like to knock the stopper out. Bump! And the dashing and the swilling have stopped, and you are sure something has given way, and that the bottle is to be emptied. But no; on they go again, bottle-washing, churning, pitching, rolling, until you are delighted to get down and thank your Maker afresh that He has given you powers of locomotion on your own account. When the roads are rough, and independent stumbling goes on between the mules, it is almost impossible to describe the variety of experiences that the traveller comes through.

About seven o'clock we reached Wang-yüan, the place where we were to spend our first night. The driver took us into the courtyard of the inn in grand style. Soon there were some strange shouts in the yard; and the inn-helpers came forward and lifted the little wooden saddle, which is attached to the shentzŭ, out of its place in the pack-saddle on the mule. The now docile animal in the front, as soon as relieved of its burden, walks off briskly to the nearest manger. The men then set down the foreshafts on a trestle, and set free the rear mule in the same way. Now the observed of all comes out of his cover, somewhat cold, certainly hungry. Some one shouts at somebody to dust a room for the great foreign gentleman, and a man rushes to the place indicated. With a little bamboo scrubber he raises such a dust that it is quite out of the question to wait till it has fallen. Our room opens from the common hall; but it has no door. With characteristic readiness and slipshodness the servants bring two leaves of a door, and pop them into the sockets. By-and-by, however, when I try to shut it, I find it impossible—it was never meant for this doorway. No chairs, no table, not a stool was in the room. The only article of furniture was a narrow rickety bedstead with a few stalks of the tall millet stretched across. An earthen floor; black, black walls; the place where the window frame used to be, stuffed with straw; rafters festooned with the sooty cobwebs of ages—there you have a true picture of my bedroom, dressing-room, dining-room, and reception room (all in one), not in black and white, but in black only. With not a little fuss a table fourteen inches high was brought in. Oh, it was dirty and greasy—the Chinese do not use table-cloths. I was hungry, however, and the table after all was too insignificant a thing to come in between a hungry man and his supper. After supper, I had some interesting conversation with quite a number of men, and was fairly comfortable under the circumstances. It turned so much colder as the evening went on, that soon I crept into bed, minus my boots, hat, and jacket only.

CHAPTER II

IT is not a pleasant thing to turn out at 3.35 A.M. under the most favourable circumstances; what shall we say, then, about doing so in a Chinese inn on a frosty morning, just when one has commenced to feel comfortable? It has to be done, however, as the muleteer says we must have an early start in order to get into a good line of villages and inns. I was very thankful for a cup of hot cocoa that my servant got ready for me before starting. The morning was keen, the road rocky, the darkness as the dawn drew near was most intense. The flickering light, from the paper lantern carried by the muleteer, seemed to make the blackness blacker: it cast most grotesque figures on the rocks by the wayside. The mules were fresh and rushed on—it is a rush in the morning, whatever it may be in the afternoon. One would think, to hear the animals stumbling a little on the stony road, that each long-eared helper was the happy possessor of twice the usual number of legs.

By eleven o'clock we had done sixty-five li, and arrived at Tao-ts'un, a place having a considerable market, which is held every five days. On the way, we passed through what must be delightful scenery during every season but winter. Trees, mountains, streams, little villages nestling here and there, made up at times even in that December weather most pleasing scenes. People were running from all points to have a look at me. Oh! for the power to direct them to look off unto my Saviour!

A market was being held at Tao-ts'un, and I thought it my duty to walk through the place in order to help the people to get accustomed with the appearance of foreigners. It was most amusing to see a tall fellow, about six feet, running after me just to have a look. He had been in a butcher's shop when I passed, and had been standing critically weighing in his hand a piece of meat. He came up at my right side, with the meat still in his hand, and passed me about four yards, eyeing me so intently that he was almost slipping into a cesspool. Then he passed to the other side of the street, and went back to his buying with a look of intense satisfaction, shouting to those whom he met, "I have seen him." The butcher, determined looking, and carrying a cleaver that he had just been using, was coming after the tall fellow to get from him the price of the meat. The customer grinned broadly when he met the butcher looking solemn, and exultingly assured the man with the cleaver that the foreigner was worth seeing. The "man with the cleaver" saw the humour of the situation, and joined the tall fellow in a hearty laugh. It was ridiculously funny to notice the looks on the people's faces. Every one was very friendly.

In the evening we arrived at another market town, which, I felt, was quite open to receive the Gospel. Again I had no door to my room; but a little bit of matting was nailed up, and served the purpose very well. After having eaten we had a number of visitors, to whom my teacher and I told the story of Jesus. They listened most intently, and asked many questions which showed an intelligent interest in the subject. One man said that he had a book at home, and that he would go and read; he had tried before, but could not understand. I gave away a large number of tracts there. One of them, "The Forgiveness of Sin's Plan," seemed to take hold. Long into the night I could hear some of the occupants of the inn talking the matter over, every one assenting to the fact that if this plan were true it was very simple, very easy.

. . . .

"Blessed are ye that sow beside all waters;" that was a comforting and strengthening word on which to step out this morning. After proceeding about forty li we could see the famous millstone quarries of Lai-yang. To-day I had one of those little experiences that knock great theories to pieces. I—being a man of peace—have always advised quietness and coolness in any sudden. emergency. Well, about nine o'clock this morning I was sitting, or rather reclining, in my shentzŭ, and being bottle-washed, churned, swilled, and I do not know what more, when at an exceptionally rough part of the road (?) the back mule fell. The saddle slipped from his back, and the front animal pulled away at the shentzŭ. My heels were so much higher than my head that—well, it was not pleasant. And didn't that leading mule pull! Gentle reader, I put it to yourself: if you suddenly found yourself being hauled along the dry bed of a rocky stream in a cart without wheels, and with your heels in the air, do you think that that would be a fair time for testing your theories? My experience squashed my theories, and almost knocked the corners off some bones. And oh! how that wicked mule pulled! I seem to feel the bumping now. We soon got the saddle put right, however, and went on our way, rejoicing that nothing more serious had happened than the scattering of a few theories.

About noon we arrived at Lai-yang, and stopped at a good inn in the north-east suburb. Lai-yang is beautifully situated in a valley among the hills, and is surrounded by trees.. It is a well-built city, having substantial walls, and having numerous ornamental arches in its streets. It was the eastern terminus of an old canal which dragged its enormous length through the centre of the province. The district is noted for its pears, wax-trees, millstone quarries, and gold.

After having partaken of an excellent meal of bread and butter, potted beef, and tea, I had a large number of open-eyed, open-mouthed visitors — all very friendly. They listened most attentively while I tried to tell them of a mighty Saviour. There was an old man present who seemed to understand me perfectly. After I had spoken a few sentences I stopped while he explained to the people; then I spoke a few more, and so on. It was difficult to leave such an interesting and friendly audience. I got my teacher to change some silver, and we left the inn about 1.30, going right through the city as we held straight west for P'ing-tu-chou.

I saw to-day one of the most amazing structures in temples that I have yet seen. There is no doubt that the priests in China are wise in their day and generation. Their temples occupy the very best sites in the land. In selecting those sites they keep several objects in view. They must be somewhat retired: that speaks of self-denial and withdrawal from the world. If a freak of nature can be added, so much the better: the ignorant people will be the more easily impressed. The temple Wang-si-

WANG-SI-MIAO TEMPLE.—*Page 15.*

miao was the most striking I have seen. Some of its outer buildings looked as if they were really hanging over the mountain side so far that they were practically courting destruction.

After leaving Lai-yang the land on every side was very poor. The Saw-teeth Mountains were still very conspicuous, and further to the west of them we were catching hazy glimpses of the ranges to the north-east of P'ing-tu. We had many opportunities on the road of speaking to numbers of people who had never heard of that Name we love. Every one was willing to listen, but we had time only to sow a little seed here and there. Village after village where the name of Jesus never had fallen from human lips! It was truly hard work to pass them by. The American Presbyterian missionaries and others have worked and are working round this district, and doing noble work too; still there are tens and hundred of thousands here who know not that there is a Saviour.

A little after six o'clock we arrived at Shui-k'ow-t'eo, having made 125 li for the day. This is the largest village in Lai-yang district, and has the most commodious inn in which I have yet been. It has a large market every five days, and would be a splendid centre for work. To-night my man made some rice ready, and was delighted with his success when he was able to put before me whole three courses: (1)

with Liebig's extract and a little tea poured in = soup; (2) with condensed milk = pudding; (3) with jam = dessert. We had quite a number of visitors this evening again.

Next morning we got off about six o'clock, and after the first ten li had a fairly good road. The cart ruts commenced here, and from this point they grew deeper and deeper.

Now every combination of yoke is to be seen: a horse and a mule, a horse and an ass, a mule and an ass, an ox and an ass, &c. I saw two oxen, two mules, and one horse, yoked together, dragging a heavy cart along. To-day we crossed two rivers with some little difficulty. At the first one, down which there was a quantity of ice floating, the mules refused to go over. The muleteer tried to get on the back of the leader and so get across, but that mule was unwilling. By-and-by the shentzŭ was led back from the bank about fifty yards or so; then the muleteer said something into the ear of "that mule," led him up to the edge of the water, and shouted till the traveller got safely to the other side. The driver had to go two li down the stream to get across at a narrow foot-bridge. So here I was in the shentzŭ with those animals, pleasing themselves to their heart's content.

Once while I was walking to-day the leading mule fell at a little stream; the rear mule followed suit.

How Pateo, the muleteer, stormed and raged at his animals! He cursed them. He cursed the spirits of the ancestors dwelling in them. Bitterly and sarcastically he deliberately addressed them, "Ni puh shï lo-tsz; ni shï k'éo," the literal translation of which would read, *You not are mules; you are dogs.* The front mule got up and shook himself, glad to be relieved of his burden if only for a little while; but the rear one got himself in between the shafts of the shentzŭ, which was now lying on its side. My belongings were in beautiful confusion. How calmly the passers-by looked on! By-and-by we got things put right—Pateo scolding and cursing all the time, and those mules standing with a most penitent and desponding air about them—and went forward.

As we went along I got into conversation with a bright boy with a fine face. He was the only one of all the passers-by who had helped to pick up some of our things at the breakdown, and was going in the same direction as ourselves. At a certain part of the road here, I almost forgot where I was. A blithe little lad, with his basket over his arm, was telling me that he was going to see his aunt; that his mother had told him that if he were treated well he might stay for a day or two, but if otherwise, he was to come home next day. On he prattled after the first shyness was off. And what was in his basket? Oh, only a small present of candies and sweet bread for

B

his cousin, and something for his aunt and uncle. Listening to a home-like talk such as this, and hearing the larks singing gaily overhead, might well make one forget where he was for the time being. We told the lad of Jesus' love. What wonder and amazement seemed to possess him! Before parting with him we gave young "Brightface," as I called him, a copy of the Gospel, and prayed our God to bless the precious word.

We saw several herds of swine to-day, with the men attending them. My teacher had never seen a swine-herd before. As we went along we talked for a long time of the Prodigal Son, and of the return home.

While we rested at Yüen-hsiang, about 11.30, we had splendid opportunities of preaching Christ. The people as a whole treated me very well: some frowned; but I think that, by God's grace, we helped to smooth away the frowns. Drs. C—— and N—— were asked for in a very kindly way. Two hours after, we were on the road again. In several of the villages through which I passed, the children were quite excitedly shouting to one another, "The give-book man has arrived." They were mistaken, however, as far as I was concerned; for I do not believe in the indiscriminate giving away of books to the heathen. This afternoon, for the first time on my journey, have I heard the cry of "Foreign devil."

About fifty li more and we reach Ma-lan, where we put up for the night. After a fair night's rest, we started again at six o'clock on a good road. Eight li to the west of Ma-lan we crossed the White Sand River. Although the river banks were two hundred yards apart, the water itself was not more than thirty yards across, and very shallow. In the rainy season the river is troublesome on account of its being so wide and rapid. About sixteen li to the west of Ma-lan, we went off the road to visit a spring enclosed in an octagonal wall in front of a temple. The place is known as Sheng-shui-ch'ï, *i.e.*, Holywater Pool. Before leaving Chefoo, we heard that the force with which the water kept boiling up would prevent a cash from sinking if thrown in. We polished three cash on the stone wall, and, throwing them in, watched in vain for their reappearance.

Just before arriving at P'ing-tu my attention was drawn to a temple known as the Tsien-fuh-ko—the temple of a thousand idols. My teacher, Mr. Ü, told me that they had gods there for every conceivable object or subject. He had heard that, even like the Athenians of old, they had something set apart for any god whom they might have inadvertently overlooked.

CHAPTER III

EARLY in the forenoon we reached the suburbs of P'ing-tu. I called upon two American ladies who are, I believe, doing a noble work in that district. A large number of people followed Mr. Ü and me to the door of the house where the foreign ladies lived. After long delay the door was opened, and we stood and talked for some time, but did not go in. The Chinese say enough of evil things about foreigners without any show of reason; had I gone into the house of the two ladies mentioned, they, the ladies, feared that such a step might have harmed the work in P'ing-tu. Under those circumstances, as I turned away from the door, I could not but feel that I was a stranger in a strange land. The ladies may have been quite right, but it seemed to me to be a poor lesson to the Chinese, as to how to treat a brother in the Lord. I carefully explained to Mr. Ü the position that the ladies took up, and put the best face on it I could, but he seemed dumb with astonishment at the seemingly inhospitable treatment.

P'ing-tu-chou is, perhaps, next to Wei-hsien, the most important city in Lai-chou-fu. It is in the centre of a fine wheat-growing district, exporting which commodity to wealthy Huang-hsien. The straw braid is still an important industry, though prices have declined heavily of late years. In the city itself shoes are manufactured, and exported to Japan by way of Chiao-chou. Bean oil and beancake are also sent in various directions. The chief trade is with Wei-hsien, the imports being largely from that region. The gold mines, about ninety li from the city, can be reached by holding seventy li to the north-east, and then due north over a bad road. During the latter part of 1890 the mines were shut down, but operations were renewed in February of the year following. Foreign engineers have had charge, and the work is being done with foreign machinery.

On we went, in a westerly direction, along a very pleasant road. One could not fail to observe the peculiar looking little heaps of earth in the fields. I was both instructed and surprised to learn that these were made by the people as they were gathering the hua-seng, or what are known in the West as pea-nuts. The plant grows to the height of one foot, then the flower comes. By-and-by the flower droops over, growing all the time. It burrows itself in the earth, and its seed develops into hua-seng, "flower life," or "flower produce." At the right season the farmer comes with something like a scoop and riddle combined. He scoops up a quantity of earth and hua-seng, riddles the earth out into little heaps, and gathers the nuts. The heaps, hundreds of thousands of them, made one think of a great battle-field, or an extensive cemetery.

We rested this forenoon at a place called Mên-Ts'un. The landlord was most affable. He was interested in everything we said and did. He asked many questions which showed his intelligence. He counted it an honour to have had the privilege of waiting upon the great foreign nobleman. He hoped that the illustrious foreigner, if passing that way, would again call in at his unworthy abode and honour it by his presence. Then the voluble rascal finished up by demanding twice the usual charge made on travellers like myself. Mr. Ü paid him the ordinary price with an air that did not admit of discussion, and we were soon on the road again.

The dialect in this district was most difficult to understand. Indeed, I could make nothing out of it at all, and more than once Mr. Ü had to confess that he did not understand what the country people said. They looked most obtuse, and we felt quite helpless in trying to present our Saviour to them, so we presented them in prayer to the Saviour. Part of the district through which we travelled had suffered severely from floods during the previous year. The land was very poor, the people poor and wretched. There was not a country school for 100 li, the people being too poor to provide a teacher. Some boys and men followed our mules for ten or twelve li to gather manure on the road. Not an ounce is left on the way, as the fields require all that can be got.

It was dark before Ma-chia-chuang was reached, so we halted there for the night. My sleeping-place was a wretched hole, all too close to a cess-pool. A four days' market was to commence on the day following, and as a number of excited merchantmen had taken up their quarters already in the inn, the noise was not little. The division between their room and mine was made of quarter-inch boards, with a good many cracks in them; and, poor though the boarding was, it did not extend all the way to the ceiling. Those fellows were having a gay time of it. They gambled; they told stories to one another; they boasted terribly; they played practical jokes on one another; they expressed great hopes or fears as to the market on the morrow—each one speaking at the pitch of his voice. Now one of the hangers on about the inn comes in among them. He stoops so badly that his head and his feet look as if they must meet soon. His staff, which was merely a bamboo, four feet long, reached to about the height of his head. His appearance at once suggested to some of the merry fellows the idea of a bow and arrow —the bow being minus the string.

"Well, Mr. Stringless-Bow," said one, "have you eaten your rice?" The man addressed frowned, but did not speak.

"Oh!" exclaimed one of the others, "I have heard a good story of what a bow without a string can do."

As most of those round him heard the word "story," they prepared themselves to listen. Soon there was perfect quietness on the other side of the thin partition. We, on our side, also got the full benefit of what was told. The story-teller held forth in something like the following:—

"On one occasion a very proud fellow was riding along the road, in a district which he did not know. In a field by the roadside he saw a man, bent with years or with hard toil—perhaps with both—who could not straighten himself up. The proud rider, seeing the strange curve of the man's figure, not condescending to use common courtesy in asking the question, and not careful whether he should hurt the man's feelings or not, said to the bent toiler—

"'Well, old Bow-without-the-string, am I on the right road for Pi-ta-chow?'

"'You are not on the right road at all,' answered

Chinese at their Best, Sunday.—*Page 24.*

the insulted man, raising himself as far as his infirmity would let him.

"'What must I do, then, old Stringless-Bow,' said the proud one, 'in order to get on to the right road?'

"'Go straight over the top of that mountain,' replied the labourer, indicating a high range at some distance. 'Look down into the valley on the other side. Look for a road there: that will help to put you right.'

"The rider went off without a word of thanks or a good wish. He toiled up the mountain side, although there was no road there. He dismounted and helped to pull his horse up some of the worst places. When he got to the top both horse and traveller were almost ready to fall.

"Eagerly he gazed down the other side of the mountain and across the valley. There was not the least appearance of even the narrowest path. A precipitous pathless descent, and a valley beyond full of immense boulders, formed the scene upon which he gazed disconsolately. One glance told him that he had been sent on a fool's errand. There was decidedly no road in that direction.

"The ascent of the mountain had been difficult, the descent he found much more so, and dangerous, too. The pony got his hind-quarters peeled, and the proud traveller had his fine shoes spoiled on the rough stones. At length, however, he got back to the road he had left, and, far on the afternoon, indeed almost towards the time of the evening meal, very hungry and very angry, he came to the old man who still stood stooping over his hoe.

"'What did you mean, old Bow-without-the-string, by sending me away on such a fool's errand?' thundered the man, who used the nickname.

"'Oh, ho! you have come back,' smilingly retorted the labourer. 'The Bow-without-the-string yet managed to send you to the top of that mountain. Be very thankful, foolish young sir,' said he, 'that I had no string. If I had had a string I would have sent you right to the foot of the mountain on the other side. Learn to speak respectfully to men so much older than yourself. You asked me to put you right, and I have tried to do so. Ride on, young sir, you are on the straight road to Pi-ta-chow. You were on the right road at first, but you asked me impertinently to put *you* right. May you travel smoothly.'"

After having heard the story, the one in the company who had first given the deformed attendant the nickname, seemed to have felt some twinge of conscience, or some fear concerning the morrow's success, and thinking that he should make some amends, said to the offended man, "Teh-tsui ni lao ren kia," which really meant, "I have sinned against you, old man," and the other looked satisfied. On the noise went again. While we were having worship (in Chinese, of course) they quietened down. A large crowd soon collected in our room and round the door. They quietly listened to the singing of our evening hymn, and stood wonderfully still while Mr. Ü, my servant, and I read in turn. (Pateo, the muleteer, did not commit himself to the one party or the other.) We knelt for prayer, and Mr. Ü led. Then I prayed, and when we got up from our knees the Chinese looked about them in such a way as gave me to understand that they would not have been surprised no matter what uncanny thing had there and then appeared.

Saturday, 20th December.—Up we got at three o'clock, and off as soon as possible, hoping to make Wei-hsien the same afternoon. The road was, on the whole, very good. After proceeding about eight li we crossed the Chiao-ho, afterwards called the Hsin-ho. Thirty li further on we reached the Huai-ho, which we crossed by ferry. The water was not more than forty yards wide, although the bed of the river at the place we crossed was more than 300 yards. We arrived at Wang-lu at ten o'clock, rested, and had our morning meal there. Between nine and ten I had a very pleasant surprise. We were making our way west with as much expedition as possible, and paying little attention to the barrows, chairs, carts, &c., that we were meeting, when out from among the shouts of drivers and yellings of chair-coolies I heard myself named in English. To say that I was filled with surprise expresses but very feebly what I felt. It seemed to me as if I had been hurrying along in a dense mist, and that out of the mist a voice came naming me. It was easily enough explained, however. A couple of foreign missionaries were on their way down to Shanghai—one of them *en route* for England— and they had heard from the natives that I was on my way up to the capital. We had a brief, friendly chat, and then, commending each other to the Father's care, we set out again, refreshed by the brethren in a way that stay-at-home people know nothing about. And then we were in the mist again.

Twenty-five li to the west of Wang-lu the road to the Wei-hsien foreign houses leaves the great road at Han-ting. At 4.15 we sighted the buildings, and were soon in most comfortable quarters in the house of Mr. F. C——. The friends at Wei-hsien, with their usual generous hospitality, made me feel quite at home.

.   .   .   .

What a luxury to have a thorough good bath, and a whole night and morning in a large roomy bed, such as I had that night! The day following I looked over the little foreign village at Li-chia-chuang. The American Presbyterian Mission has there a piece of ground, 350 yards by 100, with a good many buildings, two of which are two storeys in height. But what a time the Mission had had before it found itself stationed at Wei-hsien! One of the missionaries, in writing me giving an account of the opening of the station, says: "An epidemic of smallpox broke out about the time of our settling in the village, and Mrs. M—— was compelled to go to Ch'ing-chou-fu until the new house was sufficiently advanced to allow a room to be occupied. Great annoyance was caused by unprincipled workmen. The first set of men who had been engaged were summarily dismissed. This caused great indignation. In order to get revenge they joined with some mischievous persons to hinder the work. They threatened the lives of those who were afterwards employed. Shots were often fired in through the windows where the foreigners were supposed to be. Placards were posted up giving notice that on a certain day the foreigners would be killed. Small huts, which were put up for the use of the workmen, were burned down. Watchmen were frightened away, and none could be found who would dare to take their place. To their other duties the missionaries added that of armed night-watchmen. Many nights they spent thus, encamped on a pile of lumber, until the disaffection gradually wore away. Beyond the excessive worry, however, and exasperation incident to these riotous proceedings, no serious damage was done. Only those who have passed through it can fully realise the anxiety and vexation of such an experience. By request the local magistrate issued a proclamation, which had a wholesome effect in quieting the people. Among other admonitions he reminded them that 'If one foreigner were killed, ten would come in his place.' The people adopted this sensible view, and, rather than have their country over-run with 'foreign devils,' accepted the situation."

There is a great deal of machinery here ready for good work in the evangelisation of China. Nay, there is a splendid work already being carried on. The school for the sons of Christian Chinamen seems to be prospering, and from this centre mighty influences must be radiating. I heard a good address from the school teacher from the text, "I am the way." He treated it in a thoroughly orthodox manner, and now and again warmed to his subject, even though the church was wretchedly cold.

Wei-hsien is a most important city, with a population of 100,000, suburbs included. It is justly famed for the quantity of paper it manufactures and sends out. As a Shantung market it stands third. Goods are brought from Chefoo in great quantities, and on market days they are distributed over a large extent of country, principally to the south. The principal products of the county of Wei-hsien are wheat, millet, and beans; but all kinds of vegetables raised in North China are grown. Coal—a soft anthracite—abounds. Mines are worked about forty li from the city. Several years ago some foreign machinery was imported, but it has not yet been put into use.

CHAPTER IV

WE left the Mission premises on Monday, 22nd December, and held north-north-west towards the city. The Mission buildings, as I have said, are in the village of Li-chia-chuang, about five li from the city. In Wei-hsien itself there was no direct mission work going on at the time I visited. Indeed, of all the places I have yet been in China, I felt that foreigners were hated most heartily here. In passing through the suburbs I had some very bitter things said to me. I was most forcibly reminded that I was indeed a stranger and an alien. So I did what good I could by the way and pushed on.

Away to the north not a hill was to be seen. It is so smooth that in the summer the residents at Li-chia-chuang feel the influences of the sea breezes. Twelve li to the west we crossed the Hsiao-ü-ho, and six li further on the Ta-ü-ho. Midway between Wei-hsien and Ch'ang-lo there is a great work carried on in limestone. Many barrows, I noticed, were loaded with the raw stone, but the greater number had burnt lime as their load. The barrows were often pulled by small donkeys. The barrowman, from his place between the handles, with a strap round his shoulders, a long whip convenient to his best hand, and his mouth full of maledictions, steadied his ever-swerving one-wheeler and urged forward his assistant, Neddy, constantly reminding that assistant of the vile traits of former ancestors, and of the awful death that he, Neddy, must surely die if he did not attend to his business.

Poplar trees are much more numerous than I have seen them on my journey. We have passed through some deep cuttings, and the road is wearing deeper and deeper into the fresh-water deposits so plentiful here. With much curiosity I picked up a few shells from the beds of streams. Here, too, there were innumerable, strangely shaped nodules sticking among the deposits mentioned. At first I took them to be flint, but on breaking one or two found that they were not unlike baked clay. At three o'clock we passed through the town of Ch'ang-lo-hsien, a small place, and apparently of no great importance. The scenery was very tame. As I have already said, there was not a hill to be seen towards the north. By-and-by a low range began to show itself in the south-west, conspicuous upon which was the temple T'ai-kung-miao, situated on Ku-shan.

After getting over seventy li we halted at a place called Yao-kou, and spent far from a comfortable night.

C

This inn was indeed a miserable place to be on a road of so much importance. There was no door to my room—but we get accustomed with that. The partition did not go up to the roof; and somebody persisted in burning straw during the night. Kind reader, if you have never needed to be shut up in a dirty hole, full of the pungent smoke from straw which was too green to blaze but dry enough to smoulder, let me venture to suggest to you that therein lies subject for much hearty thanksgiving. I awoke about midnight with a bad fit of coughing. Sleep and straw smoke had a battle; the latter won. I tried reading for a time. How my eyes *did* smart with the smoke. And then the innkeeper's good lady every little while would shout at a dog which seemed to be sharing her room, shout in such a style as she might have done had the dog been half a mile away. I cannot say how thankful I was when the time came for a move to be made.

After having spent such a miserable night, imagine my disgust when I learned that the landlord wanted not only the usual amount for travellers, but wanted money for firewood (he had already been paid for "hot water"), money for the shentzŭ standing in the "hotel" yard, &c., &c. We got off gladly about six o'clock, and went along at a good speed. Part of the road to-day was through quite a swamp. Immediately after leaving Yao-kou, we crossed a

splendidly built bridge and passed into I-tu-hsien. After making twenty li we crossed the Mi-ho by ferry, ourselves and the loads being taken over first, then the beasts of burden. This cost for the whole eighty cash, with which the men were very well pleased. The water is not more than forty yards across, although the river bed is not less than 500 yards from side to side.

The ferrymen were fairly kind and friendly. They eyed, however, with evident suspicion a field-glass that I carried slung over my shoulder. They said plainly to my teacher that they believed that it was a pair of revolvers. Alas, that foreigners are mostly connected in the minds of the natives with firearms and opium! As I did not wish the men to think that I would be speaking to them of the Prince of Peace, and at the same time carry weapons of war, I took out my field-glass and offered it to the head man to look through. He would not at first, as he was suspicious of some evil design. But after a time he took it, and I focussed it for him on a man about a quarter of a mile off. Amazed, the looker began to talk to the distant man in an ordinary tone of voice, and the other ferrymen did not know what to make out of it. Of course they must all have a look, as nothing dreadful had happened to the head man who looked first. Although it took a good deal of time, I felt that I might be helping the way for other foreigners, so I gave each of them a peep at several things. They were delighted, and I had a good opportunity of telling them of something that my teacher and I had that enabled us to see all the way into heaven. I trust they learned a lesson of faith that day that will be fruitful in after years. At length we got away, several of the men calling after us, "By road or river may you have it smooth."

To-day I noticed large numbers of mulberry trees, and so would infer that this is a silk-producing district. A very rough part of the road was travelled just before getting into Ch'ing-chou-fu. We had no difficulty in finding out where Dr. W—— lived: he has a great name in the district. The people treated me very respectfully on the way, and I could see that when we asked for the foreign doctor's house they were quite pleased. Indeed, the first man from whom we asked information, although we were a mile away from the place, at once volunteered to take us to the doctor's, telling us at the same time how he himself had been healed by the foreigner.

We have been marking the noble proportions of the watch-houses on the road sides. Often the eaves are not more than three feet high, and the ridge six feet; the end turned away from the road has been so placed that it rests on some mud-bank. Dirty, wretched dens have the wretched, dirty soldier-servants of His Majesty the Emperor, on the highway.

At some of the watch-houses there is an attempt at a flagstaff, and one passes along on his weary way puzzled as to whether he should grieve most at sight of the attempted splicing of the two knotty pieces of stick, or at sight of the dirty rag exhibited near the bowed head of the flagstaff.

We reached Dr. W——'s house at noon, and had a most cheerful welcome. At once I felt at home, and this feeling only became intensified as I stayed. The Chinese waiting-room was crowded with patients, and some one was preaching to them. There is no doubt that a splendid work is going on here. By-and-by Dr. W—— took me round to see some of the friends, and I decided to stay Christmas at Ch'ingchou. My knee and ankle had been troubling me a little, but the kindly medical skill brought to bear on them soon put me right. I went about in the Doctor's barrow, and found it a most delightful mode of travelling.

In connection with the Mission (English Baptist) there is a capital native school, from which it is hoped many young fellows will arise to be noble preachers of the Cross. The scholars are receiving a very thorough mental training. On the day I visited the school, I was amazed to find on the black board a figure connected with one of the propositions of Euclid, Book III. Then, too, there is a splendid museum that is bound to have a great influence on every one who visits it. In it there are beautifully arranged specimens from the whole district of which Ch'ing-chou-fu is the centre. I am certain from what I have seen that the work has taken good root in this city.

Ch'ing-chou-fu, the capital of the prefecture, and at one time the capital of the Province, is famous as having been the home of the rulers of the Ming dynasty. From Cloudy-Gate Mountain, three li to the south of the city, one can easily trace the old city wall, which must have enclosed a piece of ground twice the size of the area covered by the present Ch'ing-chou. In the south-eastern part of the city, there is a large space said to have been the spot where the Palace Royal of the Ming rulers stood. Beautifully carved stones are often being turned up in that neighbourhood. A little to the north-west is the site of the Snow Palace, the place where Mencius taught, being marked by two lion like animals in stone, and a slab bearing the name of the place. The city, like almost all Chinese cities I have seen, bears upon it the stamp of decay. It has no great trade, although it has a provincial fame for its cutlery and basket-work.

In a temple to the north-east, immediately beyond the city wall, there is a slab of great antiquity. It was said to be over 2000 years. I was successful in procuring a rubbing of the stone. On returning to my home at Chefoo, my teacher and I looked into the subject carefully, and I was not surprised to find that the stone was not as old as had been stated. Still it was of sufficient age to be intensely interesting: we found that it had been set up 479 A.D. — more than a hundred years before the time when Saint Augustine brought the Gospel to Britain.

Three li from the north gate of Ch'ing-chou-fu is a strong Manchu city, built in the form of a square. There are over three thousand soldiers within the walls; and there should be sixteen hundred horses. But, as the full number of horse soldiers had on no occasion been called out at one time, those in charge, with the usual cupidity of orientals, and with consciences benumbed by the fatalism of their creed, provided only six hundred horse, and charged the government accounts with the full number. This kind of thing goes on over the whole empire: officials buy antiquated, used-up firearms and charge the military department more than would have bought an equal number of the newest and best; powder magazines are filled with a damp, black something that often refuses to explode; ships that are scarcely sea-worthy figure in the navy, and the man most able and willing to bribe rises highest. It is folly; it is suicidal; and the Chinese have found this out to their cost in the recent war with Japan.

The Manchu soldiers at Ch'ing-chou-fu were strong, manly-looking fellows, and those of them with whom I talked were most gentlemanly. Just outside their city they have a splendid stretch of level ground on which to parade, and where they are expected to turn out every morning. I learned that the young lads are always practising at bow and arrow; because, whenever they can shoot the large arrow, they draw a soldier's pay. While I was out seeing this Manchu city, I beheld the novelty of a barrow being helped forward by means of a sail, and was much interested in it, as it was the first time I had seen anything of the kind.

25th December! Christmas Day!—Day of good tidings and great joy! Day of happy, holy associations! Peace on earth and good will to all men! To-day I went out to a temple near the West Gate, and there saw a Buddhist hell. What a sight it was! Some of the carved figures were represented as being roasted, some boiled in oil, tied to red-hot tubes, ground between stones, and dogs licking up the blood. The representation suggested that every demon in the pandemonium had so much business in hand that there was no time to be ceremonious. Many of the devils were depicted as having horns and a tail—not much unlike what Satan is described as in some of our western books.

In the evening all the foreigners in the city—all

missionaries—met at the house of Dr. and Mrs. W——. There we had an excellent Christmas dinner, with plum-pudding from England, no less. After dinner a most pleasant and profitable evening was spent. What stories from Scotland were retold! What rehearsals of boyish days were given! For the time being one almost forgot that he was a stranger and pilgrim away in far Cathay. At half past ten we joined together at family worship. Our loved ones in the home country seemed very near to us that night, as we claimed for them a Christmas blessing.

CHAPTER V

AFTER such a pleasant break in my journey, I left Ch'ing-chou-fu with much reluctance. At eight o'clock, on the 26th December, I set out under the most favourable circumstances. I had got some of my stores renewed; the morning was bright and beautiful; and I was to have the pleasure of having a foreign lady travelling with me for a couple of days. Dr. W—— accompanied us out to the west gate of the city, where we parted from him with much regret. In addition to our former equipage, we had now Dr. W——'s barrow. It had been designed by himself, and was most comfortable for the traveller, even on very bad roads—the wooden springs being so arranged as to break in great measure the force of the bumps.

What a delightful difference this was from my former days' travelling! We walked for about ten li, and then put all the things into the shentzŭ, ourselves taking the barrow. The reader must not imagine that the barrow spoken of was shaped after the English pattern. The principle was the same; but the wheel, instead of being so far for-

SCENE BY THE WAY.—A HEAVY LIFT.—*Page 42.*

ward, was placed near the middle of the structure, and thus received the greater part of the weight. When the load can be divided nicely it makes the work easy, as a part can be put on each side. The wheel comes up so high that the person using the conveyance can rest his arm comfortably on the top of the crate that covers in the upper half of the wheel—said crate is also very useful for clinging to at times. On the day of which I am speaking, however, everything was *shuin, i.e.*, level, peaceful, propitious. The lady took one side of the carriage, and I had the other. It was very pleasant, and would have been delightful all the way if the roads had kept good.

For some distance we went north-north-west, but kept more westerly after crossing the Chih-ho. This river-bed is two li wide. At this season there was little water in it, but in the sixth moon its average depth is four feet, and it goes about eighteen li per hour. The city Lin-chih lies to the north of the road, at a distance of twenty li. It was the capital of the Tse-kuo, the "Seven Kingdoms," and, at the present time, most interesting relics of bygone ages are turning up in its vicinity. Not very far from the Chih-ho we saw some seven or eight great earth-mounds, in which we became intensely interested. They were pyramidal in shape, and marked the ancient tombs of princes. Although all were shaped exactly alike, they varied considerably in size. Each side of their square base would be from 50 to 120 yards long. Indeed, had their apices been higher, one would have compared them with nothing better than the Egyptian Pyramids done—as the Chinese do most things—on the cheap. Two months before we arrived at that place three men had been put to death for burrowing into those mounds and extracting some remarkable relics.

All along we notice that the mulberry trees are cultivated. They are planted in rows, and form pleasant avenues. The red date tree, too, is very plentiful; while over all the landscape dark patches of yews give a fine variety of shade. I have noted larger poplars to-day than I have yet come across. We meet hundreds of barrows and carts, all heavily laden—coal from Po-shan, and crockery from Chih-ch'uan.

The hill known as Niu-shan was a conspicuous feature in the landscape this forenoon. It is forty li north-west from Ch'ing-chou-fu, on the south bank of the Chih-ho. This is the place spoken of by Mencius in Book vi., part i., chap. viii., where he moralises thus: "The trees of the New mountain were once beautiful. Being situated, however, in the borders of a large state, they were hewn down with axes and bills; and could they retain their beauty? Still through the activity of the vegetative life day and night, and the nourishing influence of the rain and the dew, they were not without buds and sprouts springing forth; but then came the cattle and goats and browsed upon them. To these things is owing the bare and stript appearance of the mountain, which, when people see, they think it was never finely wooded. But is this the nature of the mountain? And so also of what properly belongs to man; shall it be said that the mind of any man was without benevolence and righteousness? The way in which a man loses his proper goodness of mind is like the way in which the trees are denuded by axes and bills. Hewn down, day after day, can it—the mind—retain its beauty?" and so on. But we must leave Niu-shan.

At another point on our journey to-day, I had an instance of the importance of general information on the part of the traveller. I have hesitated whether to speak of it here or not, for fear that I should be misunderstood. But even at the risk of appearing to make a parade of the little thing, I think I should mention it. I do so the more readily because I hold strongly to the idea that there are very few things that a boy or man learns at home that he will not make use of some day should he ever travel in a land such as China. For example, it never occurred to me when a boy that when, for amusement, I learned how to milk a goat, this very ability should go to help to save the valuable life of a missionary many years after. But to return: as my teacher and I walked along together I saw oozing out from a hillside some water which, though brownish a little in colour, gave a yellowish tinge to the stones in its course. I remembered having seen something very like it near my village home in Ayrshire, Scotland, and concluded that there was probably iron ore in this hill.

At a spot where the road cut a little into the hill I lifted up a piece of stone, and, unobserved by my teacher, tried what effect it would have on my pocket compass when held near enough. The stone was a piece of highly magnetic ore, and fairly made the needle dance, even when held a little way off. By-and-by I said to Mr. Ü, my teacher, that that was a valuable hill we were passing. He looked surprised. I asked him if he knew the name of it; but he did not. Jokingly I said to him that the foreigner would tell him: the hill should be called the "Magnet Hill." He was respectfully amazed, but agreed that I should know. I picked up a piece of sandstone from the roadway, and showed him that it did not influence my compass in the slightest, and then showed him what a piece of the hill stone could do. He looked at me, but said nothing for a little while. I could see by his face, however, that he was deeply impressed; and the muleteer, who made no profession of being a Christian, seemed to say by his looks, " There must be something in this religion, after all. Here is a foreigner who knows far more than our own teachers, and he believes in it. There must be something in it." I could notice that my companions in travel looked upon me even with more marked respect than they had done before, a respect that was intensified when my teacher, on asking a passer-by the name of the hill we had just left, was told that it was called the " Iron Hill."

At noon we rested at a place called Hsin-tien and partook of our mid-day meal, adding no little to the general excitement. At the time we arrived there was a large funeral in progress, and the whole village seemed to be out of doors. When the foreign lady and gentleman sat down to eat, they were speedily surrounded by the wondering crowds. They by-and-by tried to preach the Gospel to the gaping multitude, but there was too much noise and stir.

After a little we set off again, doing fifty li as the second stage of our journey, that is 100 li in all— very good travelling, seeing that we had started so late in the morning. For part of the evening the moon was beautiful, and we had splendid light, but great banks of cloud began to rise from the west, and soon the sky was overcast. A little after eight o'clock we drew up at an inn at Chang-tien, and before very long betook ourselves to our rooms. That was a very poor night for me. I had got a bad cold before reaching Ch'ing-chou-fu. Under the kindly treatment I had had there, however, I seemed to have got rid of it. But I had not. During the night I slept none. I was troubled with a nasty cough, and severe pain in the chest. The morning threatened rain, but as the distance to Ts'ou-p'ing was only sixty-five li, and the roads would be bad for days after if rain did come on, we resolved to go forward.

On reaching Ch'ang-shan-hsien, a distance of forty li, we rested, cold and wet. After waiting for two hours we went on again. The roads were now almost impassable—certainly not easily described. We did not meet more than half-a-dozen people for the next twenty-five li. My teacher lost his shoes in the mud: my lady companion and I fared badly. When we arrived at Ts'ou-p'ing we were quite knocked up—I had walked the last twenty-five li. Immediately I got to bed, and did not get up next day. Mr. and Mrs. N—— (English Baptist Mission) kindly entertained me, and did everything in their power to make me comfortable. Mr. J——, of the same mission, not only acted as medical adviser with marked success, but gave me much exact information concerning his large district. Snow came on next day, and I did not leave Ts'ou-p'ing till the 31st

SCENE BY THE WAY.—OFF ONCE MORE.—*Page 49.*

December. Although this is a hsien city, it is a very poor one, with broken-down walls, and a generally dilapidated look about it. But yet it is the centre of a splendid missionary enterprise which is bringing forth much fruit to the glory of God. It only remains to add here that my lady companion soon recovered under kindly treatment, similar to what I received.

And now let me finish this chapter by giving the translation of an amusing story I heard from the Chinese at Ts'ou-p'ing. In that part, if one Chinaman wants to say that another one is almost too stupid for anything, he says, "Tsao teng t'ui." Now that means, "He searched for a leg for the stool." And how that came to be a byword was in this wise: A half witted servant lad was sent out by his master one morning to the woods to cut a leg for a stool. (Readers must understand that the shape required would be like the letter Y turned upside down 人; a piece of the single part of the stem would go up through the stool.) The lad took the axe with him and did not return till it was dark, and when he did appear he did not bring what he had been sent for. The master was angry, and accused him of being blind, or lazy, or stupid, and really he did not know what he had been doing all day.

"Did you go to the woods at all?" said the master.

"Oh yes, master," was the reply; "and I searched diligently from morning till night."

"And did you see no clifts like that at all? Surely you must have seen something like it?" said the master.

"Plenty! plenty! hundreds!" cried the youth with the axe; "but they were all turned the wrong way—the clift was up instead of down."

"Aw! aw!" was all the master said. What more could he say to such a servant?

CHAPTER VI

As the lady who had travelled with me for two days was going no farther, I once more pushed on alone—as far as foreigners were concerned; still, my Chinese teacher made a very pleasant, chatty companion. On the last morning of the year we set out from Ts'ou-p'ing about 7 o'clock. The roads were rough on account of snow and frozen slush. From 7 till 9.30 o'clock we held south-west, and then west till nightfall.

About twenty li after leaving Ts'ou-p'ing, we came on a large body of water, almost worthy of being called a lake. It had formed some two years previously at a time of flood, and had refused to leave. The frost had been keen for a couple of days. At the time we passed, a large number of Chinese were evidently enjoying themselves on the ice. The morning was crisp and frosty, the sun was shining brightly: the different coloured dresses of the Chinese gave a gala aspect to the whole affair. The people looked like so many children at play; but we soon found that they had work on hand as well. They had made holes in the ice, which was transparent. In moving round about these holes they would spy a fish. Then they would prance and skip about it till they got it right under one of the openings, when, with wonderful dexterity, they would spear their prey with a sort of trident, and soon have it safely in their baskets.

At eleven o'clock we rested at an inn in the southern suburb of Chang-ch'iu. I felt very tired indeed, as I had been walking all the morning, and up to this point we had covered fifty li. After about an hour and a half we held on towards the capital. Soon after leaving Chang-ch'iu, at a narrow place on the road, we met a cart; and our muleteer making a dash at the bank, led on the front mule, but the rear one stumbled and once more got rid of his burden. I was walking at the time, so I did not come in for a bumping. Something about the harness was broken—a straw rope probably—and it was some little time before we were all on the move again. Not long after we met another cart in a very deep, narrow cutting. It seemed quite clear that the cart and the shentzŭ could not pass. My muleteer and the carter looked at each other "with murder in their eye."

"Didn't you hear the jingle of my mule bells?" shouted the carter.

"Where were your ears that you did not hear me shout to you to wait?" yelled Pateo in reply.

There those two men stood for a quarter of an hour

within three feet of each other, yelling out questions and insinuations—yelling as loudly as they would have required to do if they had been a quarter of a mile apart. I am glad to say that my vocabulary of vituperative Chinese is very small: it seemed infinitely smaller as I stood for a little in the presence of those giants in the art of reviling. Ancestors were consigned to the most terrible fates; with appropriate gestures, children and children's children were cursed roundly and heartily right on through coming ages.

Not wishing to hear all the discussion, I walked on ahead, believing that nothing serious would follow the service of malediction. Of course I advised them as to what I thought should be done—my muleteer was clearly in the wrong in not having mule-bells on his animals. After about an hour my company overtook me, and I asked Mr. Ü what had happened after I had left. I learned that the two men had kept at the strong language for a while. Then they had got out their pipes for a smoke. Pateo had got fire from his flint and steel first, and gave the carter a light. They had had their smoke, saying very little the while. Then, as if moved by the one thought, they lifted the shentzŭ from the backs of the mules, and held it up angled in such a way against the side of the cutting that the cart got scraping past. They got the shentzŭ on to the mules again—the carter helping cheerily; and the two men, who at one time looked as if nothing would satisfy them but blood, parted with smiles and good wishes.

To-day we saw very many date trees. I notice that as I get nearer to the capital the better-class looking people get more scornful in their looks. At four o'clock we were within some fortifications which were at one time intended to surround the space on which the capital of the province was to stand. The shentzŭ after this had to go through some extra steep cuttings. I went a different road on foot, and in about an hour and a half we came together in a large important village, where we spent the night. Since our resting time I had walked other fifty li, making in all for the day one hundred li. The roads had been very heavy, but I hoped that the day's walking would help me to get thoroughly over the effects of my recent cold. I need hardly say that I was tired—I scarcely cared what the place in which I tried to sleep was like.

1st January!—Happy New Year! dear reader, and best wishes—among the wishes, one that you may never spend such a night as I did in the inn in Lung-shan, known by the euphonious name of the "Eternally comfortable." A pig that had probably been sleeping in the sun a good part of the day seemed to have scented out the "foreign dog" about 2.30 A.M. The brute had pushed the door open as she came in, but the leaves of the door had swung to behind her. I do not think I had been sleeping at all up to this time: indeed, I felt as if I was too tired to sleep. Well, that pig skirmished around to its satisfaction. My bed was about a foot and a half from the ground. How playfully that brute gambolled after each sniff of the "foreign devil." With some little effort the foreigner got hold of his walking-stick, a good strong one that had been lying near the foot of his bed. On the first opportunity the key-note was struck, and that old sow set up such a tune as roused the house; indeed, in some of her mad rushes, she looked, more than once, as if she would bring down the rickety building altogether. By-and-by the landlord came and drove it forth—I am glad to say that he used language that I did not understand. As he drove it out in a kindly sort of way, the only two words I caught were "ma" and "tsong." The former means "curse," and the latter "ancestor." One of the men secured the door properly, and soon all was quiet with the exception of the old sow; she seemed to murmur and sob until it was time for me to get up. And the name of the inn—"Eternally comfortable!"

I found on getting up that morning that the walk of the previous day, and the broken night that I had just experienced, had been no good preparation for my first visit to the first city of the Province, on the first day of the year. I got into the shentzŭ at 6.30 A.M., and we set off to make the capital without halting, if possible. Sometimes I walked, and at other times I was cooped up in my litter. By this mode of travelling one is cast much upon their own thought. The jolting and shaking put reading almost altogether out of the question. The limited view becomes depressing—the rear quarters of a mule; two ears that might almost pass for wings, and which seem, on account of the traveller's position, to be growing out of said near quarters; the back of the muleteer's head; a peep of the sky now and again—the whole framed in as it were by the front arch of the shentzŭ, you would not say that that was an enlivening scene, especially after you had suffered from it for many days. Under such circumstances one's thoughts, cast back upon themselves, would often lead away into higher subjects, and times of earnest prayer and sweet communion would be enjoyed. But often, on the other hand, and especially for a time after a breakdown, one is apt to sit with nerves braced up ready for a crash, as they constantly seem to be on the very

A City Gate.—*Page* 57.

verge of dissolution. If a cart be coming in the opposite direction, the muleteer and the carter hold on their way till it is almost too late, and then get off as by a miracle.

The people began to get more numerous on the way as we neared the city. The roads were terribly cut up. The sun had melted the snow, and the people waded complacently along among the mud. About one o'clock we neared the city's approaches. All around the suburbs looked nicely wooded. Not infrequently now do I hear it bitterly said just behind me, "Foreign devil." Often on my journey I had heard children calling out such things to me, and thought little about it; but here even old men do not seem to think it beneath them to engage in such sport: the laughter at times from young swells sounds anything but pleasant.

The eastern suburb is quite as large as some of the cities I have passed through. It has a good wall on its own account. Just as we passed into the east gate of the city proper, under the very arch of the great city wall, "that rear mule" again collapsed, and the traveller's heels were once more much too high for his idea of comfort—he is not an American. He scrambled out of the shentzŭ as quickly as he could, much to the enjoyment of several score of people, who gathered so rapidly that they looked as if they had sprung out of the ground. Think of how quickly a crowd gathers in the Strand, London, or at the corner of Argyle Street and Jamaica Street, Glasgow, and it will give you some little idea of what soon happened. There we were in almost semi-darkness under the low arch of a wall at least ninety feet thick at the base. In two minutes there was a great line of vehicles blocked behind us, and several hundreds of people were getting amusement at the expense of the "foreign devil," whose mules refused to take him into the noble city. Such a state of matters demanded instant and energetic action, and that action was forthcoming. Pateo took the head of the leading mule, the servant took the tail of the rear one, the teacher put his shoulder to one side of the shentzŭ, and I put mine to the other; and I think "that rear mule" almost staggered with surprise at the speed with which it was hurried into its burden. I was truly thankful when we got out of our trying predicament.

It is remarkable how the traveller is cheered by the sight of foreign products in the country, and of foreign merchandise in the town. Here in passing along the streets I saw large quantities of foreign cloth, lucifer matches, kerosene oil—known in Chinese respectively as yang-pu, yang-ho, and yang-yu—at sight of which the yang-kuei, "foreign devil," did not seem to feel so far away from home.

As Mr. N—— of Ts'ou-p'ing had given me directions as to where I might find friends, we had no great difficulty after we were fairly within the great Chi-nan-fu. First I called at Dr. N——'s, and on there learning that Mrs. M——, of the American Presbyterian Mission, had very kindly prepared a room for me, I was soon at my destination, and very comfortably and happily settled. It was exceedingly pleasant to get into such congenial company. The missionaries had their usual prayer-meeting that night in a certain part of the city for all foreigners; but as it was at some little distance from Mrs. M——'s, they kindly advised that as I had such a bad cold I should stay at home, and so be more likely to get about afterwards. This I gladly agreed to, and got some of my notes written up. By-and-by sleep seemed as if it would quite overpower me. After a luxurious bath and wash, and a very thankful time before the Lord, I tumbled into bed. And such a bed! roomy and restful, and with sheets like the driven snow for whiteness. It had a spring mattress: didn't I enjoy it!

I am sure that was the most peculiar New Year's Day that I have ever spent. Once or twice, just when I was almost over to sleep, I gave a great start, with the horrible thought that I was being shut up in some dark underground passage, and being buried beneath hundreds of shentzŭs. Again I would see millions of Chinese laughingly putting their arms into holes in the ice and pulling out enormous fishes, which, on being brought fully to the light, proved to be duplicates of "that rear mule"—all held by the tail!

CHAPTER VII

CHI-NAN city is to Shantung in importance what London would be to England if Oxford and Cambridge were added to the metropolis. It is not only the capital of the prefecture in which it stands, but of the Province. Distant from Peking some 960 li, it is situated near a bend on the eastern bank of the Yellow River, which is twelve li to the north, and forty-five li to the west. The city has a population of at least 515,000, which may be thus divided: 1st, acting officials; 2nd, ex-officials and graduates awaiting office; 3rd, resident gentry, generally people of means and education, and of great influence; 4th, middle classes, such as doctors, teachers, priests, merchants; 5th, skilled workmen; 6th, servants, soldiers, and unskilled labourers; 7th, beggars—and the number is large. Among the population there are said to be 15,000 Mohammedans. The city is blessed, or cursed, with seventy yamens, or magistrates' offices. Residing within its boundary there are the holders of the following posts: Provincial Governor, Provincial Judge, Provincial

Treasurer, Intendant of Circuit, Provincial Examiner, Prefect, and City Magistrate. I might mention as the sights of the city, the Roman Catholic Cathedral, the Mohammedan Mosques, the great springs, the lake, and the residence of the Provincial Governor.

In this city there has been a good deal of trouble now and again between the foreigners and the Chinese. Seldom, however, is it the common people who stir up strife; nor is it, as one might expect, the priests. These latter are often poor and ignorant, and with little power among the people. But it is at the door of the literati that the blame must be laid for nine-tenths of the disturbances that have occurred. I have not witnessed anywhere, among men supposed to be educated gentlemen, such bitterness and spite as I saw and experienced in the proud, literary capital of Shantung. The fop dressed in silks and satins, flipping his sleeves close to the face of a respectable foreign visitor met in the street; the middle aged scholar dressed as a gentleman, not thinking it beneath him to hiss out "Foreign devil," or "Devil;" young and old spitting on the ground in bitterness, close to the visitor's feet, laughing right in his face, or, on passing, turning sharply round and making a most hateful noise at the stranger's ear—these are specimens of the petty annoyances, that some of the literati and gentry practise: underlings easily carry on the treatment to something more serious.

Now, let me tell you about the Roman Catholic Cathedral. As far back as the time of the Emperor Kangshi (1662), the Jesuits had got a grant of this land on which their buildings now stand. Although driven from the country, in the time of the great persecution, immediately on the passing of the decree of 1860, they re-appeared on the scene, and presented their title-deeds, which could not be gainsaid. The cathedral was built in 1861. It is at least fifty feet high, and has a most imposing appearance in a heathen city. Inside, the walls are covered with frescoes of fairly good quality—the product of native talent. The only painting by a foreigner is that on the ceiling, in which is depicted Adam and Eve being turned out of the garden of Eden. Along the left hand wall on entering may be seen three pictures of bold conception. The first one is to represent hell, the second purgatory, and the third heaven. As the Cathedral is connected with the Franciscan brotherhood, St. Francis occupies a position to the right on entering. In the building there is very little room for worshippers. The two-storey houses in the rear give excellent accommodation to the fourteen or fifteen priests, who pass their time there. I had a glance into their library, which was but poorly stocked:

my attention was also drawn to their printing press.

Would you like to come with me out to the southern suburb, and see how this great city is supplied with water? If you do come let me warn you before you set out that the pavement of the streets is very irregular, that the mud pools are numerous, that the beggars are worse than importunate, the city arabs awful, and the gentry rude. Still you think you will come: very well; let us set off.

So off we set through one street that seems to be given up to booksellers, through another where only cutlery can be seen; after that we have the crockery street, clothes street, sweetmeat street, and so on. No, no; I do not wish to explain to you all those remarks that the two grandly dressed young men were making: some of them were rude. But here we are at the outlet of the subterranean reservoir. Three great natural springs supply the half million people in Chi-nan-fu with water. Those springs are not less than a foot each in diameter. Of course they are constantly pouring forth a stream of beautiful clear water: the pool in the centre of which they boil up never freezes. No, you don't like this jostling. I do not blame you; let us go back.

In the northern part of the city there is a pretty lake some three li by two in extent. The water comes from the springs in the southern suburb, and is always clear and fresh. There are many narrow roads crossing and recrossing this lake. In spring and summer it must be beautiful, with its miniature house-boats passing and repassing, the lotus flowers in abundance, the tall reeds bowing to the passers-by who, clad in their many coloured costumes, sit under the awning of their dainty boats sipping the fragrant and refreshing tea. The water from the springs and lake finds its way to the outside of the city by the north gate, which is not used for anything else but a water way.

On the 3rd of January, accompanied by Mr. H—— (American Presbyterian Mission), I set off after lunch for a walk to the thousand-idol temple on a hill a few li to the south of the city. It was a very testing walk, but we were well repaid for having taken it. To see the carving on the sides of the hill quite made up to us for any labour we had gone through. But there, with my field-glass, we could see at our feet the great city with its half a million souls; and there to the north, twelve to fifteen li, like a great, broad, yellow band laid down, stretched the wilful Huang-ho, or Yellow River. There, too, we could see Lo-K'ou, the port for Chi-nan-fu, and we could easily distinguish the sails on the junks in port. Looking down upon the city from our elevated

E

position we seemed to see only an enormous collection of temples and yamĕns, with some magnificent pagodas standing out here and there. The domes of the Mosques in the south-western district were also conspicuous. And one could not fail to notice the great space covered by the Governor's residence.

As we came down the hill we turned aside for a little while to look at the foreign cemetery. It was not closed in in any way. Three mounds and slabs told us the story. The centre one spoke of the pioneer missionary of Shantung, Rev. J. S. M'Ilvaine; the one to the west held the sacred dust of little Jeanie Drake, daughter of one of the missionaries of the English Baptists; while that to the east covered the remains of my companion's wife. How my heart ran out to him as he told me of his great loss! Only five weeks in China, and his dear helpmate was stricken down: only one short week's illness, and she was gone from him, and laid away on the lone hillside. As they had carried the body through the streets to put it away in its resting-place, hell's most virulent fiends seemed surely to have been let loose in Chi-nan-fu: the mocking laughter, the jibes, the yells of "Foreign Devil," "Devil," "Dog"—all came back to him vividly while we stood by that grave, although it was years since she was left under the nodding cypress trees which overlook this demon-possessed city.

On the day following I saw another sight in heathen Chi-nan, which affected me greatly. I went to a gathering of Christian Chinese, and there beheld some eighty men and fifteen women meet together to worship the living and true God. What a witness that was to the power of the Truth! Almost a hundred Chinese meeting together on the Lord's day in the centre of a city the most hostile to Christianity of any city in which I have ever been! The view we had had from the hillside the day before had been something to move one; but HE who looked down from the battlements of glory saw in that Chinese gathering a sight that thrilled heaven itself.

I had a good, long rest that afternoon, and in the evening I had some liberty in a talk with the missionaries on the third chapter of Philippians. But now my pleasant and instructive stay in Chi-nan is drawing to a close. My kind host and hostess urge me to remain with them a little longer, but, with many thanks I decline, as I feel it to be my duty to be moving on.

The history of the rise and progress of mission work in Chi-nan-fu has been an eventful one, owing to the long-continued and intense opposition on the part of the gentry and literati of the city. This opposition has not been a persecution of Christianity as such, but a result of the jealousy and distrust existing throughout China against foreigners in general. It has taken the form, for the most part, of a determined struggle to prevent missionaries from renting houses, buying land, or erecting any permanent buildings. For eleven years this contest has been carried on; for the labourers, while intensely desirous of being allowed to tranquilly pursue their work of evangelisation, felt that buildings for residence, chapel, hospital and dispensary, for native evangelists, for inquirers, and for schools, were absolutely essential to the success of their work, and so have been compelled, most unwillingly, to maintain the struggle.

This opposition has culminated in a number of riots. In 1881 a partially built chapel was demolished, and Messrs. M—— and H——, with their families, were forced to take refuge in the Tao-tai's (chief-magistrate's) yamĕn. In 1887 the school was threatened by a mob of several hundred people, which was, however, dispersed before working any damage by the prompt appearance of the local magistrate on the scene. In 1888 Mr. R—— was maltreated by a mob in the southern suburb; and in the year following, Mr. H—— (English Baptist) was beaten by a crowd in his own rented house. Besides these several overt acts of violence, there have been at various times rumours of riots, which happily were never actually realised, but which often gave the missionaries times of much anxiety. On these and other occasions, natives having dealings with the foreigners have been cruelly treated in the yamĕns and by the mob—one man, who was guilty of nothing but selling the missionaries a piece of his land, died in prison from exhaustion, caused by starvation and beating. This opposition has not been popular, but has been instigated by a few influential residents of the city, who, by bribes and threats, have induced others to join them in the movement.

Notwithstanding these obstacles, however, steady progress has been made; and workers must be thankful for that as they remember what China is. There is no mission field in the world seems to me to be so difficult as China is. Nor is it to be expected that a civilisation of a character so wholly exceptional as that of China, which has been the slow crystallisation of ages, should yield rapidly to any influence from without. It is scarcely to be hoped, even, that a province which boasts itself as the birthplace of the great sages of the past should readily accept a faith which is destined to throw the teachings of those sages into a rank greatly inferior to that which they have hitherto occupied. But the results already accomplished by the Gospel, even in this idol-loving, literary capital, are regarded, by those most thoroughly cognisant of the facts, as at once a prophecy and a promise of what the Gospel may reasonably be expected, in the fulness of time, to accomplish, not only for this city and this famous province, but for the whole of China.

CHAPTER VIII

WORDS fail me as I try to describe the sense of freedom that I experienced that morning when we got fairly outside the unfriendly city on our way to the tomb of the great sage. It was a delightful relief to get away from the squalid streets and the sickening smells, the pertinacious beggars and the insolent respectability, and to find myself once more out in the open country—albeit I knew not what might await me at the next inn at which I might put up. I had not observed that I had been under such depression till I got right away from Chi-nan. But as I went along the road I could almost have shouted out with real buoyancy of spirit. Perhaps the foreigners living in the city get accustomed to their surroundings—and I hope they do, for their own sakes—but although I knew that the people were not friendly, I did not care to judge, nor was I really able to do so, of the strain which I had been undergoing until I had been right through it. There can be no doubt, however, that the realisation of the fact that one is surrounded by, and walled in with, half a million of his fellow-beings who detest him, who openly and superciliously insult him at every opportunity, and who would gladly see his death accomplished, must, if he has been observing his position, feel an almost indescribable sense of relief when he suddenly feels himself outside this circle of unpropitious circumstances. So I felt soon after we were clear of the western suburb.

It was almost ten o'clock by the time we found ourselves in the open country. We now held southwest, having a fine range of hills close to the road on the left. Limestone was in great quantities in this district. By 11.30 we had precipitous hills on both sides, and did not get out from among them all day. As we had bought a good many things at Chi-nan-fu, the shentzŭ was pretty well loaded, so for thirty li to-day I rode a donkey. Pateo made the bargain for the hiring of said animal. I wish I could let my readers hear anything like that bargaining. What skill and scorn my muleteer displayed as he belittled the donkey offered for the "great man's" use! What surprise and amusement the possessor would have us believe he was deriving from the ignorance of Pateo! And there stood the strong, nimble-looking animal seeming withal deeply dejected. After half-an-hour the bargain was struck — though for the last quarter of an hour the owner of the donkey was walking with us while he talked —

his animal coming on behind at a kind of Paddy's trot.

The bargain having been clenched, it was time for the great foreign gentleman to take his seat. If the "great one" remembered aright, the last time he had ridden a donkey was when he was about the beginning of his teens, and on that special occasion he had been forced to assume a very lowly position, much more summarily than he had anticipated. But he must not stand and moralise: he must mount.

I had grave doubts about the angular points of that pack-saddle before I got on my charger's back. Still, they seemed to be covered up pretty well, and I hoped for the best. Alas, for human hopes! Before I had gone many li, what had appeared as only most obtuse angles were now so acute, that I found it necessary often to change the points of contact or impact. For a long time I sat in the ordinary way, astride; then I tried one side, and afterwards the other. Still the angles grew more acute. At length I removed the saddle altogether, spread a mat on Neddy's back, and got along famously to the distance agreed upon. Of course the owner of the donkey did not go with us all the way. Our muleteer carried a message to a friendly innkeeper at the end of the thirty li, to say that the donkey was to be hired back if possible to its master's house. If a hirer did not turn up it was to be sent back on the following day by itself: it would easily find its way home. And what had I paid for the donkey? One hundred and fifty cash, equal to about eightpence of our money.

For the rest of that day's journey, fifty li, I walked. We did not rest anywhere, as we had set out so late, and we purposed if possible sleeping at a place called Chang-hsia. About half-past five we reached our destination, and were thankful to get into an inn of any kind. Although Chang-hsia is the largest market town in Ch'ang-tsing-hsien, has a market every four days, and boasts a resident magistrate, the inn which we got, and which was said to be the best in the town, was something awful.

Next morning we got away about half-past five and began at once to hold south by south-east. After proceeding some twenty li we came upon a man selling sweet, hot potatoes. It was very pleasant to get one in each hand on a cold, wintry morning; but we did not let them get too cold before we ate them. At nine o'clock we had our first glimpse of the mass of mountains, of which T'ai-shan is the highest point. For a long distance our road ran along the bed of a stream. It was very rough on the mules, the rear one often seemed as if on the point of rebellion. Sometimes our way led us well under the immense overhanging cliffs, and again we were descending rapid, rocky falls.

We rested at Tien-t'ai for our morning meal. Although it was a very small village, soon there were gathered about us two or three hundred of a crowd. After our rest we set off refreshed, still holding in a southerly direction. The li seemed to get longer as we got near the capital of the prefecture, but I walked to the end of our day's journey, 110 li. As we got near the city I could not fail to notice the splendid boulders of grey granite by the roadside, and the temples on the towering mountains towards T'ai-shan. We arrived at T'ai-an-fu about half-past four.

In the south-west suburb I saw an extra large cavalcade of camels. The animals were in the courtyard of a camel inn. Some were ladened and ready for the start; others were in the act of kneeling to get the burdens placed on their ungainly humps, while others were still resting quietly, preparatory to the long night's march. I was told that camels were allowed to travel along the great roads by night only. When they proceed by day they cause a perfect panic among the ponies, mules, and donkeys; and they literally clear the high-roads as they quietly pass along. A very eerie feeling crept over me the first time

I met one of such cavalcades. It was in a narrow gorge, about six o'clock on a wintry morning. I had not heard any sound to indicate that anything out of the usual was approaching—the camels carry no bells. Suddenly they loomed up in the semi-darkness; swiftly and silently they passed by and seemed to melt into the gloom with their strange looking loads, themselves so strangely shaped, and looking many times their natural size, so noiselessly and so unexpectedly had they come upon me.

I must confess I was very tired after my walk of thirty-six English miles. I soon got to the head-quarters of the Church of England Mission, and had a hearty welcome from Mr. B——, the only worker at home. After a most refreshing tub I had a pleasant evening with my host, who gave me quite a stock of information concerning the great mountain and the surrounding district.

T'ai-an-fu stands at the base of T'ai-shan, and annually reaps a rich harvest from those who come to worship at the sacred mountain. Combining business with religion, few of the pilgrims of the poorer class return to their homes without taking with them some of the famous pien-tangs or carrying-poles and large wooden forks which are sold in the city. It is also famous for its beancurd, cabbages, and water: even young children in T'ai-an, when asked what their city is noted for, answer in a singsong manner which gives to the reply the air of a proverb:—

"Fei-cheng li, Lai-wu mei,
T'ai-an, teo-fu, peh-tsai, shuei,"

the translation of which would go to say that the city, Fei-cheng, is noted for pears, and that Lai-wu is noted for coal, but that T'ai-an boasts of beancurd, cabbage, and water. What gave the city the greater part of its importance, however, seemed to me to be its proximity to the well-known mountain T'ai-shan—a paragraph on which may not be without interest.

The Chinese have five particularly sacred mountains. T'ai-shan is known as the Tung-yo, or east peak. It is second in height of the five, the summit being 5050 feet above sea-level, and is looked upon as the most sacred. This peak is mentioned in the Shu-King as that where Shun sacrificed to heaven (B.C. 2254). It is accordingly celebrated for its historical as well as its religious associations. It towers high above all other points in the range, and is a great rendezvous of religious devotees. Every sect in China, perhaps, has temples and idols scattered up and down the mountain's sides. There priests chant their prayers, and practise a thousand superstitions to attract pilgrims to their shrines.

During spring the roads leading to T'ai-shan are almost blocked by the long caravans of people coming and going—coming, to accomplish their vows, to supplicate the deities for health or riches, or to solicit the joys of heaven in exchange for the woes of earth; going back to their homes to wait in hope, in fear, in doubt, in sorrow, for the answers which never come.

Dr. Williamson, in his "Travels in Northern China," gives a graphic description of the scene. He says: "A plan of the hill and city gives a poor idea of the beauty of the place. If the reader, however, causes his imagination to fill the city with streets and shops; the causeway up the hill to the top with rows of beautiful trees on each side; the hills with trees, brushwood, verdure, and rocks piled rugged and threatening, with waterfalls here and there; temples of gaudy colours; and strings of pilgrims, old and young, men and women, marching up in Indian file, with richer men among them in mountain chairs; small companies sipping tea at the several arches; beggars lying on the road, like bundles of living rags or animated sores, with beggar children following each company of pilgrims, he will have some idea of the bewildering variety of the scene."

From what Mr. B—— said concerning the cold on T'ai-shan in the month of January, I decided not to go up, but to continue my journey southward next day towards the famous tomb.

As we went off in the morning we had a splendid view of the mountain. When I first turned my field-glass upon it the sun had little more than touched the summit; and as I stood and watched I beheld a transformation scene that far surpassed anything I had ever seen. What looked like irregular and fantastic clusters of rugged peaks and boulders seemed to evaporate or to assume the most divers phases of form as soon as the shafts of morning light were driven in among them. Steep, bare escarpments, wet with the breath of night, gleamed like polished silver in the morning sun. Even the most crabbed crag, with brow wrinkled, scarred and dotted, with surly, jagged shoulders, and with breast riven and cleft with many a deep ravine, softened as the new day's splendour met his gaze. Not only was there transformation in form, but in colour: pink and purple, yellow and green, vied with each other until they were left pale and white.

Looking from the distance at which I stood a deep intense stillness seemed to hold the mountain, and almost overcame the onlooker. Once and again so marked was the silence, that I could almost fancy I heard the rush of the spears of light as they darted into some gloomy cavern and put to flight the darkness. Little wonder if a designing priesthood had selected such a mountain to help them to impress the throngs of superstitious pilgrims. There is a mystic influence about mountain scenery that scarcely ever fails to draw one's thoughts higher than the mountains. It is little wonder, then, that such scenes can be skilfully used to intensify an awe-inspiring superstition in the minds of the ignorant and irrational devotees, who, time and again, crowd T'ai-shan's narrow pathways.

We held on our course the whole day almost due south, and rested for a short time to feed the animals at a place called Ta-wên-k'ou. There the people were very troublesome, and seemed as if determined to have a quarrel. We got wisdom and grace to bear with them, however, and were soon on the road again. Immediately to the south of this place we crossed the Ta-wên-ho by a strong stone bridge. Rising to our left were the Tsu-lai-shan, and away to our right were many ridges, none of them reaching any great altitude. Straight before us there was, what seemed to be at a distance, an unbroken range; but as we approached it fell apart here and there, and showed the way to regions beyond.

I was often complimented to-day by travellers going in the opposite direction. It is quite a polite thing to do on a Chinese highway on meeting a stranger to ask him where he is going. Very often a few sentences like the following would form the whole conversation :—

"Sien-seng tsai-na-li-k'ü?"
(The gentleman where go?)
"O shang Chu-fou-hsien k'ü."
(I up to Chu-fou go.)
"Kong-hsi, Sien-seng! Hsuin feng, hsuin lu."
(I congratulate you, sir. May your journey be smooth and peaceful both by water and road.)

They no doubt thought that, in some way or other, my journey would bring added respect to their great teacher Confucius, whose dust lies buried near the hsien city mentioned: hence the congratulations.

The darkness began to fall just as we got into a place called Nan-i. There we had a very trying time. Nobody would take us in: a most troublesome crowd had gathered round us: we could not get the shentzŭ turned in the narrow street—altogether we were in a bad fix. At length Pateo noticing a wide door, and which he fancied to be the door of an inn for barrowmen, dashed in with his mules and shentzŭ, and refused to go out again. Of course I followed. A wretched hole was cleared of some rubbish, and we had a roof over our heads once more. I had to lie on the clay floor that night: there was no brick bed, no door, no table, no stool even. But I got the muleteer to buy a bottle or two of straw, and we tried to be as thankful as possible. On entering, one had to step down into

F

the place, so it may be understood that more comfortable quarters might have been had. I do not think I slept more than two hours, and in the morning I did not feel anything like at par. During the night a gale of wind sprang up from the north, and the dust in our den was whirling about very thick. I shall soon be turning my face homeward again, and I shall not be sorry. To-morrow we hope to get on early to the great grave.

About 5.30 A.M. we left Nan-i with no regrets, and hurried on, getting in sight of the city of the tomb at noon. Eight li from the north gate of the city we crossed the classic Ssŭ-ho, along the beautiful banks of which Confucius and Mencius had rambled as children, and where, after many years, they had taught and exhorted their fellow-men to follow after righteousness. We got to the eastern suburb of Ch'ü-fou about one o'clock, and soon after set off with a guide to visit the tomb of the sage. But we must honour the place by giving it a chapter to itself.

CHAPTER IX

CH'Ü-FOU-HSIEN, thirty li to the east of Yen-chou-fu, and one hundred and sixty from T'ai-an, is noted as containing the Temple of Confucius, which is said to be one of the finest in China, and as having his tomb in its immediate vicinity.

Eight li to the north of the city, as I have already said, we crossed the classic Ssŭ-ho on our way south, and were immediately in the village Shu-yüan, the college, where the followers of the great sage study. Over to the north-east lay the natal village of the philosopher; here was the river on the banks of which the famous scholar used to play. One might have grown sentimental, if not poetical, on such classic ground, but as I was somewhat hungry, and had still eight li to go before resting, I stuck to my mules instead of mounting Pegasus, and hastened on. Having put up at an inn in the eastern suburb, I was soon prepared for a visit to the burial ground held in such reverence by the mass of the Chinese nation.

I am much tempted here to give an account of the life of Confucius. But as I could not do anything like justice to it inside a couple of chapters, I feel that I must refrain. This I do with the less regret, seeing that the life of this wonderful scholar has been treated so exhaustively by many able writers. Let a brief quotation here suffice in order to give substance to the shadowy name of one who lived in the sixth century before the Christian era: "No character in history is less mythological than Confucius. He is no demi-god, whose biography consists chiefly of fables, but a real person. The facts of his life, the personal aspect of the man, the place where he lived, the petty kings under whom he served, are all known."

On leaving the north gate of the city, we see a fine avenue of trees and ornamental arches extending just one li due north. At the northern end of this avenue is the entrance to the burial ground.

When we arrived at the closed gate several dirty-looking guides, poorly dressed, looked coolly on my teacher and me, as if they were calculating how much money they might manage to get out of us. "The great foreign gentleman just arrived may freely walk into the grounds without ceremony," said the wily rascals; "yet for friendship's sake the great man may present to the mean guides and keepers a trifling ten thousand cash to help them keep the grounds in good repair." At such an intimation, the said "great man," who had been warned by an innkeeper that the guides would say this very thing, and had been advised as to the answer to be given, suggested putting off his visit to a more favourable opportunity, when the important men at the gate would not be so busy—the lazy scamps had been hulking about doing nothing. At the same time the "great man's" Chinese teacher mentioned as if casually the sum of cash two hundred. Then a good deal of talk went on, during which time I was being examined most carefully. At length, after the torrent of words had subsided, the gates were thrown back with a great flourish. The bargain had been completed: the "great man" and his teacher would pay five hundred cash for admission to the sacred enclosure. The gatekeepers did not seem to think that they had done anything amiss in having demanded exactly twenty times as much as they really got.

Here we were, then, on a fine broad avenue with a high brick wall, and a row of splendid cypress trees on each side. This avenue was about twenty-five yards wide, and a hundred and fifty long.

As we marched along our guide drew our attention to what seemed to him to be something wonderful—a tree, the trunk of which had divided into three almost equal parts about four feet from the ground. My teacher, too, seemed to see something passing strange in this, and looked contemplative. On arriving at the end of the avenue, we passed through a great doorway in a wooden palisade, highly carved, and entered upon more sacred soil. Passing a temple with a fine bell, we had a scene before us which reminded me very much of the common old willow-pattern to be seen on plates. A short distance to the left, and then we held straight ahead again. But at one point here there was a closed door, and we had paid five hundred cash in order to be allowed to see all that was to be seen; so we expressed our views to the guide, who in one breath told us that the place was private, that there was nothing of importance within, that he had lost the key, &c., &c. At length a man was shouted for from another part of the grounds. He arrived, leisurely climbed a tree, got on the wall, down on the inner side, and by-and-by we heard him roll away a great block of wood which had been doing duty as a bar—so much for method. We viewed the dank and musty corners and the dead leaves, and, sighing, turned away.

. . . .

But now we draw near the sacred mound. We ought to meditate. Ah! here is a hall, a place for meditation; there, another in which the worshippers prepare the sacrifice; and yet another where aged pilgrims rest their wearied limbs. A pavilion, erected about 1750 by Kien-Lung, is pointed out

to us. Our attention is also drawn to a tree which was said to have been planted by Confucius. It is dead now, of course, but the root is built into a circular stand of stones and mortar, and the trunk is still to be seen. Close beside this is a slab of stone which looks like marble. We were told that a devoted follower of the sage had worked for long years smoothing this stone, and that when it was quite finished there was discovered on its surface an exact representation of the dead tree. There we saw it as a hard, yellow substance in the stone, but how inlaid or how produced we did not know. As we get nearer to the honoured grave, we pass along between two lines of animals cut in stone. Lions and tigers are here; nameless animals, half-dog, half-frog, are at our side; and beasts are here the like of which have never lived on earth, in sky, or sea. The sphinx, or something similar, is represented. Just at the entrance to the last enclosure stand the statues of two wise men of the past, one on each side of the road. Twice as large as life, they poise on lofty pedestals, looking solemn as a funeral, as if to remind the worshippers that here was no ground for merriment, no time for gaiety, no place for thoughtlessness—more solemn, most solemn.

Through a finely-decorated pavilion, and soon we stand beside the grave. A mound, say twelve feet high, protects the honoured dust of K'ung-fu-tzŭ (Confucius). Gnarled oaks and stately cypress trees are growing all around, and daring shrubs are creeping up the mound itself. Before this mound a tablet stands, some six feet broad and sixteen high. Upon the tablet are inscribed the name and deeds of him who lies beneath—Chih-shêng-hsien-shih-K'ung-tzŭ, meaning The Perfect Sage, The Former Teacher, The Philosopher K'ung. Before the tablet's base is placed the sacred incense vase. Alas, alas! *Familiaritas contemptum creat!* How true! Our guide looks on unmoved at tablet, mound, and vase; at sight of which in years gone by his veneration swelled.

About thirty yards to the east of the sage's tomb is a somewhat similar mound and tablet marking the resting place of his son, K'ung-li Pai-ü, who was born B.C. 532, and died at the age of forty-nine—four years before his sire. "It is recorded that his father gave him the name Li (carp), in celebration of a present he had received of a pair of fish of this kind from the sovereign of his native state." No particulars of his life are given, but it is well known that Confucius was not so satisfied with what his son accomplished, as he was with the promise which that son's son gave. The tomb of this grandson, K'ung-chi Tzŭ-Ssŭ, is fifty yards to the south of that of the sage, and is almost identical in appearance.

"The instruction he received from his illustrious grandsire became fruitfully developed by his own philosophical mind, and took shape in the treatise entitled 'Chung-Yung,' the doctrine of the Mean, which embodies the Confucian ethics in their highest form." He is canonised as one of the Ssŭ-Pei, or Four Associates of the sage, and enjoys the title of Shu-Sheng-Tzŭ, The Philosopher Tzŭ, Transmitter.

A little to the west side of the great tomb is a spot held sacred to the memory of a loving, patient follower of the sage. In early life Tzŭ-K'ung became a disciple of Confucius. It is said, that at the end of his first year's study, he thought himself more advanced than his teacher, at the end of his second year he fancied that he might be equal to his teacher, but at the end of his third he knew that he was far beneath his teacher. When the sage died, the disciples all mourned for him the recognised period of three years, but Tzŭ K'ung built a hut on this spot, and remained sorrowing for his master three years more. On being asked why his master should be regarded as a sage, he replied: "I have all my life had the heaven over my head, but I do not know its height; and the earth under my feet, but I do not know its thickness. In serving Confucius I am like a thirsty man who goes with his pitcher to the river, and there drinks his fill, without knowing the river's depth." A small building now covers the place where the disciple sat and wept; a tablet in the wall records his years of grief.

At the particular time of year of my visit, 7th January, perhaps everything was looking its very worst. I hope that such may have been the case; for a more squalid looking show, making any pretensions at all, I have rarely seen—everything marked with dirt, slipshodness, and decay. Our guide informed us that the grounds measured forty li round, but I do not think they were nearly so large. Outside the enclosed part are thousands of graves, brought as near the sage's tomb as possible. Around those graves strange sights are often seen. Men will come with paper horses, paper cows, paper servants, paper money, and will solemnly burn them at the graves of their departed friends, in the belief that those departed ones will receive the equivalents in the spirit world. Here I saw the nearest approach to a forest of oaks that I have yet observed in China.

On parting with our guide at the main entrance, we had another little skirmish in words, the subject being the great dirty-coppered, hollow-hearted god of the Chinese—cash. However, as our landlord had told us before leaving the inn that even three hundred would be a large sum to give, we parted abruptly from our quondam friend, but did so with an easy

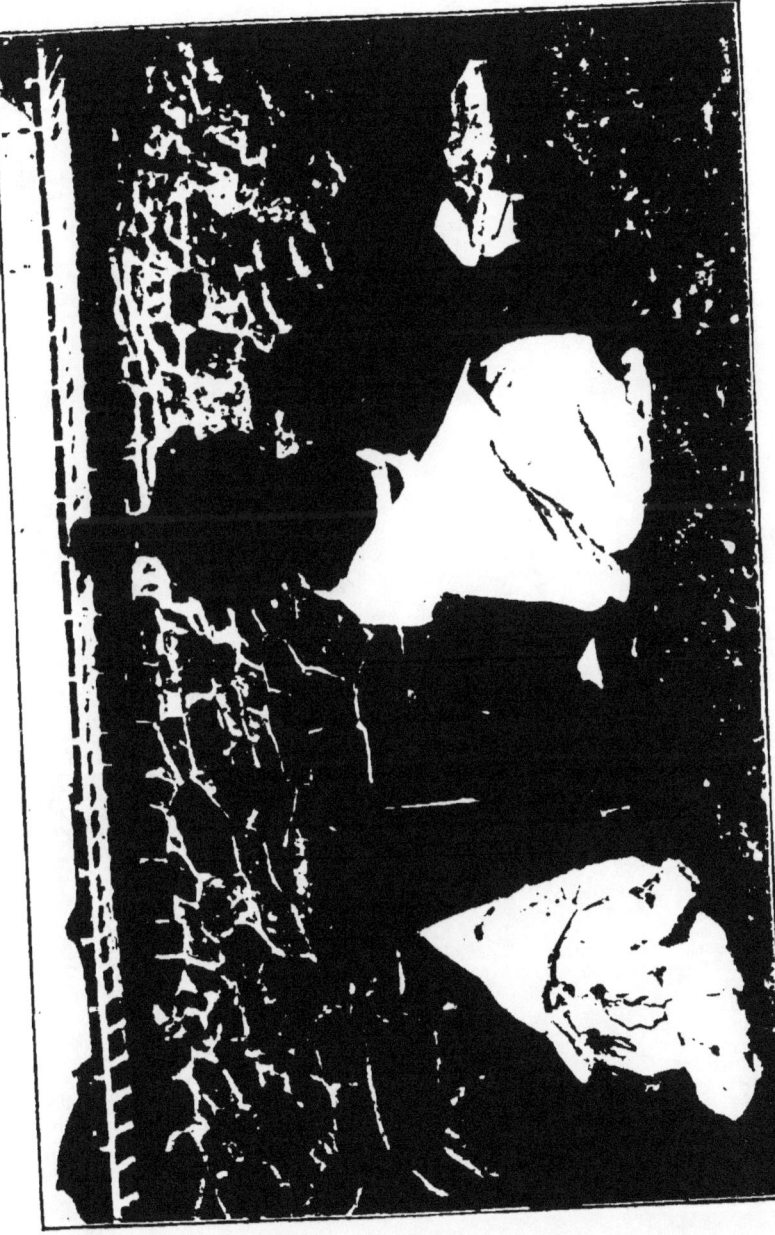

conscience. We made for our quarters, which we soon reached, saddened by the idolatrous devices we had seen, yet glad that our God had sent an all-sufficient Saviour — glad, so glad, that He had strengthened us to testify for Him.

CHAPTER X

I HAD hoped to visit the house of the descendants of the great teacher, and had a present with me for Duke Kong; but it was with much sorrow that I learned of a death which had occurred in his family only five days before. This, according to Chinese etiquette, would prevent him from receiving visitors.

Last night I decided not to go any further south. So this morning about six o'clock we turned our faces towards Chefoo once more. That rear mule grew quite lively over the event, and almost succeeded in capsizing the shentzŭ. We retraced our steps as far as Ta-wên-k'ou, when we struck on to a different road holding to the north-east. What seemed to me the most beautiful sunrise I have yet witnessed I saw this morning. Perhaps my being on the way home helped to add brightness to the general effect.

We rested at a place called Hsieh-ma-ting. On arriving, I went right into one of the rooms. But the people gathered in such crowds, and thronged me so much that I could not even get eating for them. At length I went out and stood on a chair for a little while, and let them have such a look at me as almost satisfied them. They were amazed to hear me speak their language, and listened with the greatest respect to what I had to tell them about the country from which I came, and about the happy land to which all would go who trusted their case to the Saviour. After my talk I told them that I was tired and hungry. At once a great strong fellow took up his place at the door of my room, and said that I could go in and eat in peace, as no one would enter without his permission. He made all the people laugh as he reminded them that not only was their town called Hsieh-ma-ting (the Horse rest place), but that this inn was named Man-tung (Bounteous Cavern). I had no further trouble through being crowded; and when I was leaving the place, I had many kindly invitations to "return soon, soon."

When about six li from Ta-wên-k'ou that erratic rear mule collapsed once more, probably the outcome of his gaiety in the early morning. It had often gone down before; but on this occasion it managed to give the shentzŭ such a tilt that the whole thing turned right over, the unfortunate traveller being beneath all his baggage. He crawled out from among the wreckage, and praised God that there were no bones broken. The teacher, servant, and muleteer were looking on quite scared. Some of my readers perhaps could help me to clear up a difficulty just here. How was it that there should come up so vividly before me some sentences for translation from foreign tongues into English? They were some of those ridiculous things that we once suffered from :—The horse would run. The boy must jump. Balbus will laugh. Has he seen the sister of my grandmother? Girls will weep. The poet has loved. The ass would fall—and so on.

It was an hour before we got under way again. For all the rest of the day Pateo, when not more actively engaged, was upbraiding and reviling "that rear mule." It was denounced again and again as a "dog," and an "ungrateful dog." This evening I had as magnificent a view of T'ai-shan in the setting sun as I had of it in the rising sun on my way south. But I shall not soon forget our march in the dark as we searched for a place in which to spend the night. Pateo, with characteristic frugality and improvidence combined, had not provided himself with the necessary candles for the evening. But I forgave him when I recollected how briskly even that "rear mule" had turned out and set off towards home in the early morning.

For nine li before the darkness came down, we had been making our way among low ridges of hills of granite. Here and there were deep crevasses worn by the rain of ages. Out and in among those boulders and gullies we held our way, the road (!) becoming more broken as we advanced. The servant hurried forward to try if he could see any appearance of a dwelling. Oh how that muleteer raved at that special mule!

It was pitch dark now. We moved forward cautiously; indeed, we felt that it would be serious to meet with an accident in such a place. The teacher's donkey was sent on ahead to pick out the way; but it got too far off for the speed at which the shentzŭ was going. Then the leading mule stepped on the muleteer's foot, and there was more reviling in which, be sure, the rear one was not overlooked. Things were in a bad state generally, and I felt pretty well tired.

I had just got my skin coat out, and was putting it on preparatory to having a rest, when we were surprised by a tremendous hubbub behind us. We had in the intense darkness passed the entrance to a cosy place in the hills where the village lay that we had hoped to reach. Fortunately my servant had taken the right road, and now he was out searching for us. Several of the villagers and inn people were with him. When I saw by the light of the lanterns the kind of road we had just passed over I was amazed, and increasingly thankful that no accident had occurred to our party.

Soon with grateful hearts we found ourselves in

a wretchedly uncomfortable inn in the village of Hsiao-tai-ü. The teacher found his donkey standing munching straw in the courtyard when we arrived.

Next day we held on cheerily again. I asked Pateo if he had any candles with him. Mr. Ü asked him the same question, and the servant asked him so often that in the end he took care to put some distance in between Pateo and himself before he put his interrogation. That day we rested at Chang-wên-ho, and spent the night at Chen-t'sun.

. . . .

It was a dark, cold morning when we left the village of the Chens at four o'clock. We trudged on in silence for about an hour, when it began to snow. Soon afterwards I saw what was to me a most interesting sight. Along a hillside came a whole line of lanterns of different coloured papers, but mostly red. Now and again a strange, wild sort of music would sound out startlingly in the morning air. My teacher explained to me that this was a procession accompanying some bridegroom going for his bride, or else accompanying him on his way with her to his own home.

On this subject, Dr. Nevius, in his "China and the Chinese," says: "In the province of Shantung, in the North of China, weddings are celebrated in the night, and remind one very forcibly of the Jewish marriage customs referred to in the parable of the virgins in the twenty-fifth chapter of Matthew. I once attended one of these weddings. The house was full of guests, the bridal chamber was beautifully furnished and ornamented, and everything was in readiness for the reception of the bride, when the bridegroom should make his appearance with her. We waited a long time till all were impatient, and some drowsy, and persons would frequently go out with a lantern to see if there were any signs of his coming; and it was not till near midnight that the cry was heard, 'The bridegroom cometh: go ye out to meet him.'"

About seven o'clock we met the traffic from Yen-hsin, which large place of business really surrounds the city of Po-shan. Crockery of all kinds seems to be the industry there.

After resting at a place called Ho-chuang, we pushed on as speedily as possible, as we were often hearing that there was a bad piece of road just ahead of us, and we did not wish to arrive at that after nightfall. We thought that, perhaps, we were getting exaggerated reports of the difficulty before us; but now that it is over, I must say that for once the Chinese had not overstated the danger, or overdrawn the roughness.

We came down five li of a gorge, the most terrible road surely that ever man or beast tried to foot. During the rainy season every symptom of a road is swept away, except the niches that have been worn by the animals as they have climbed the face of that precipice. We had a big breakdown at that place. For an hour previous to our arrival at the pass, we had been gradually ascending. As we neared the difficulty, bands of men came and pressed their services upon us. They described the descent on the other side as something alarming; but Pateo held forward, saying that he thought he could do without their help—he had never been that way before. After a good deal of hard work we got to the point where we could look down upon the other side. The very steepest part did not extend more than a hundred and fifty yards. On that short distance I counted eighty-four men, five mules, seven donkeys, and fourteen barrows. Not more than half the number of the mules and donkeys were standing; the loads were scattered about, the men were hauling and yelling at the fallen animals, and straining themselves over the groaning barrows. Some of the workers fairly lost heart when a full-blown "foreign devil" appeared at the summit of the pass.

We tried to make our way down, but had not gone twenty yards before our baggage donkey was lying with his hind-quarters up the hill, some of the baggage was taking the place of a pillow, and the pack saddle looked as if it were an enormous mustard plaster applied to his stomach on account of spasms —the spasms were there sure enough. Both of our mules fell, and the shentzŭ rolled over and over, our belongings being scattered on the roadway (!). A small cooking pot went clatter-clattering, bump-bumping away down the gulley. Pateo was in despair. He then called for the men who before had offered their assistance; but they would not move. They must make terms before they put their hands to the work, and they began by asking fifty times more than they expected to get. Just then Mr. Ü invited me to walk on in advance, as the men would not come down in their price as long as I was there. So off I set. Slowly and carefully I made my way along those five indescribable li, all the time doubtful as to how my men would succeed, and doubtful as to their overtaking me in time for us to get into an inn together for the night.

At the point at which I emerged from the pass there was a rest-house. I went in and sat down, when some children, who had caught a glimpse of me, set off yelling as if they had actually seen the evil one. I spoke to a man; but I used my best and worst Chinese to no purpose: we did not understand each other in the slightest. Soon they brought me some tea, and a kind of mixture that very much resembled sawdust and dough, to which, however, I applied myself. The rest-house keeper was a rough-looking specimen. He had the very look of a man who would gladly despatch a "foreign devil" just for the pleasure of doing it.

I had not a cash with me, but I had a piece of silver weighing about two ounces. I took a long time over that tea and dough, hoping that my party would appear. But at length I could dally no longer over it, and this heavy-browed, surly, murderous-looking villain wanted his cash. Of course he did not know that I had friends who were, I hoped, coming on as speedily as possible. Several people came in and looked at me, then they whispered with the ill-favoured landlord, significant looks passed between them, and they went out. I do not know what might soon have happened, but just when I felt that things were coming to a rough climax, our baggage donkey went tripping past the open door. I recognised it at once by its load. The shentzŭ was not far behind. Readers will believe me, I am sure, when I tell them that having paid my account I parted from the guardian of the "Heavenly Resting Hall" without one sigh of regret.

Our descent of the gorge made us forget all about Pateo's candles; and then we were on the way home, so we could afford to be magnanimous. As the evening wore away we neared White Pagoda village, where we expected to put up. As we got close to it some men who had been walking with us

SENDING GIFTS TO THE DEPARTED SPIRIT.—*Page* 100.

during the last six or eight li had friends come out with lanterns to meet them. We felt somewhat neglected as we saw their very kind though unostentatious welcome. I said to my teacher, just to test him a little, something about no one being there who knew us or was willing to welcome us; when he remarked in a quiet, thoughtful way, that our Father was always with us.

As we were in the coal district we had a warm kang—a brick bed with a flue through it—and were very grateful for it. I was offered opium by mine host of the White Pagoda inn. That was the first time that I had had it presented to me since arriving in China. I politely but firmly declined, and the man really looked surprised.

It was with a fierce grudge that I turned out of my cosy, though hard, bed next morning. However, we got up and away about five o'clock, steadily holding to the north-east. We had a difficulty in getting a man to act as guide in the early morning, and it was absolutely necessary that we should have one, as this was the first time my muleteer had been in the district. The man who accompanied us from the Pagoda village required three times the usual price, and even after he set out with us he wanted to give us back our money and to return to his home. Of course we would not hear of such a thing.

Two days before we arrived, the wolves, it was said, had come upon a solitary traveller on a road near the village and had devoured him. Everybody was scared. Our brave (?) guide was armed with a stout stick about six feet in length. At one extremity of it was a short chain with an iron ball at the end. As he marched along with this formidable weapon over his shoulder he looked a dangerous man. But I had a strong conviction that if the wolves had come upon us our guide would have been of little use. My mind was not much exercised on the subject, however, as I did not think wolves would be likely to attack a party of five, two of whom carried lanterns. Many a shadow was carefully examined that special morning; but we met with nothing like an adventure.

In passing through the city of Chih-ch'uan I was greatly surprised at the sight of a most unexpected turn out. There, standing in the street, was a jinricksha in good order. My teacher asked me what I would call it in my own language. I looked at it, stared at it indeed, but tried in vain just at the time to remember the name of it in English, though the Chinese name was familiar enough. I was so amazed to see a thing of the kind at such a distance from a port. Had the roads been even fairly good one might have been almost anticipating such a sight, but the roads—well, I think I have mentioned them already. This morning, too, I had another very pleasant experience; I heard the steam whistle at the coal mines, seven li to the east of Chih-ch'uan. It sounded strangely among the hills of China. I think it made me a little home-sick. I observed also a glare on the sky, just like what we have at home, coming from blast-furnaces, and learned that it was from some great kilns in the neighbourhood of Yen-hsin.

We rested at noon at a place called Fêng-ch'ui. At first the people were very much afraid of me, but I wreathed my face with all the smiles in my possession, and then fear and the lurking suspicion went out of their eyes just a little. But it is exceedingly difficult for an ordinary Chinaman to get over his suspicions. Bred as they are in an atmosphere of distrust, they put no dependence in each other, certainly have no confidence in the promises of their officials, and are ever designing how to hoodwink their very deities. I quietly and thankfully ate what was set before me, and was preparing to set out on the next stage of my journey, when a very bold man had the temerity to whisper to another the words "Wei-sien-seng." At once I was fortunate in getting hold of the thread of their thought. I told them that I had had a friend of that name.

He was very, very tall. I raised my hand high above my head to express the height, and then some of the older men fairly laughed. "Right, right," several exclaimed. "He knows him, he knows him," said others, well pleased. I then learned that no foreigner had passed through that village for over twenty years. Dr. Williamson (Wei-sien-seng) had visited it when some of the middle-aged men round about me had been in their teens: many of those in the crowd had never seen a foreigner. They soon became very friendly, and we told them of the great salvation that had been provided for sinners. I must confess, however, that they were more taken up with myself, my clothes, my boots, &c., than they were with the story of redeeming love.

By three o'clock we were again on the way. About one hour after we observed the lines of telegraph posts, and were quite rejoiced at the sight. The Chinese have got the idea that there is a little devil in every pole, and that each hands on the message to his neighbour on the next pole, as their own couriers do, stage by stage. It was a pleasant-voiced imp that sang to me from the first pole I passed. It was four weeks since I had left Chefoo, and had not had a word as to how things were at home. The music in the telegraph poles spoke to me of something else than little imps. The hill road on which we had been travelling for several days now joined the great road at Chin-ling-chin. The snow was lying deeper, and the travelling was much harder than it had been on the south side of the pass. As I had not been in the shentzŭ at all that day, I was delighted to get into even very indifferent quarters for the night at Hsin-tien.

CHAPTER XI

BRIGHT and early we set off this morning in order to have time to look in on the friends at Ching-chou-fu again; but we did not make rapid progress, as we were walking through slush and mud for a great part of the way. On arriving at the city I found that all the gentlemen, with the exception of Mr. M——, were away at out-stations. At his house I had a splendid bath. Perhaps readers smile at me for mentioning the fact; but I can assure them that a bath under comfortable circumstances makes a great impression on a foreigner travelling in the interior of China. After I had been most hospitably entertained to tiffin, Mr. M—— accompanied me out to the gate of the eastern suburb, and once again a foreign white atom zig-zagged alone amidst the yellow throng.

The roads got worse, and I became somewhat lame. Although I described this part of my journey as I was proceeding westwards, one or two little incidents happened on my homeward way, that, I think, are worthy of being recorded.

Some time in the early part of the afternoon,

while the constant stream of life was flowing past us, one man stepped out of the stream and gave me an unexpected pleasure. He was a barrowman: much like the others of the same class, who were in the way, but cleaner looking. As soon as he caught sight of me he dropped his barrow, and with a look of intense delight saluted me.

"Is the gentleman well?" said he.

"Thank you, I am well," I replied; "you are well, I hope."

"Praise the Heavenly Father I am in good health," he said, with a look on his face that told that the praise was real. "Have many listened with their heart to the gentleman while he has been out preaching the Gospel?" Readers will observe that this man, up to that time, had evidently only met with foreigners who were missionaries.

"Some men have heard as if in earnest; and many tracts and portions of the Scripture have been given away," I answered.

"Would that the disciples of Jesus were more numerous in this province," he said, in a sad tone; but added more brightly, "Still they are increasing, and we must not forget to praise for that."

After quite an interesting conversation we parted, to meet no more, probably, until that day when we shall stand together in the presence of our Master. Although he was only a Chinaman, one whom I had never seen before, and might never see again in this world, I felt my heart go out to him in a way that it never does go out to my own countrymen when they give unmistakable evidence that they are opposed to the truth. As I held on my way I looked back several times. There the barrowman stood, ready each time to signal his good-byes and best wishes.

About four o'clock, as we were hastening forward, and hoping to get across the Mi-ho River before dark, we met the old Ching-chou-fu evangelist returning to his home. I had had the pleasure and privilege of being present at a meeting at which he spoke on Christmas morning at Ching-chou, and we recognised each other at once. Although he was over sixty years of age, there was scarcely a wrinkle about the bright, beaming face. When he told me of the work he had been away doing, and how God had blessed it, such a light kindled in the old man's eyes as fairly illumined his radiant countenance. We had prayer together as we stood in the roadway, and I parted from this aged Chinese Christian with the clear consciousness that I had been the gainer through having come into contact with him.

Half-past five saw us on the west bank of the

Mi-ho, which we were to cross by ferry. Readers may perhaps remember that it was at this river that I had spent some time showing the men my field-glass. The boats were at the east side when I arrived, and the boatmen were discussing with a muleteer as to cost of crossing. I was walking on ahead of my shentzŭ. As soon as the man in charge saw me he stopped bargaining, and, calling out that the gentleman with the thousand-li eyes had returned, came straight over to me with a boat, and looking very friendly. We and all our goods were soon on the east side. When Mr. Ü was paying our fare I asked him to give the ferrymen a few more cash for the prompt way they had come and brought us across. But, would you believe it? the head boatman decidedly refused to receive one cash in excess of the correct amount. He said that he had been paid for his work, and that that was all that was wanted. "Why, sir," he said, "had it not been for the foreign teachers I would have been dead, and that man would have been dead, and that one, and that." While he spoke and referred to man after man, those mentioned showed the most perfect approval of what their leader was saying, by nodding their heads most vigorously. He continued: "We had nothing to eat, and were dying, when you came and fed us. Oh no! sir; you have paid us for our work, and we give you thanks, and trust that your road may ever be smooth."

Hundreds of times had I heard it said that a Chinaman was utterly devoid of gratitude. I knew better after that evening's experience. That man's face to me looked beautiful as he spoke. And yet, when I recollected that in every ordinary Chinaman it was supposed that the commercial instinct was the strongest one that he possessed, I looked carefully and critically at the speaker to try to make out whether it might not be within the range of possibility that this speech was intended to draw me out, and with the ulterior object of drawing out more cash. But when I again looked into his face, I was ashamed of my suspicious scrutiny. I asked Mr. Ü to press the money upon them, but they would have none of it. We reminded those friendly boatmen of the Stranger from the Far Off Land, who came, not only to satisfy them with bread in time of famine, but to give them heavenly bread, not only to save their lives, but to lay down His own life so that they through believing in Him might never die. Very, very kindly were the good-byes they spoke, and glad was I to have learned that they had not forgotten their indebtedness to the benevolent foreigners.

It was seven o'clock and very dark before we arrived at Yao-kow. Do my readers remember—it

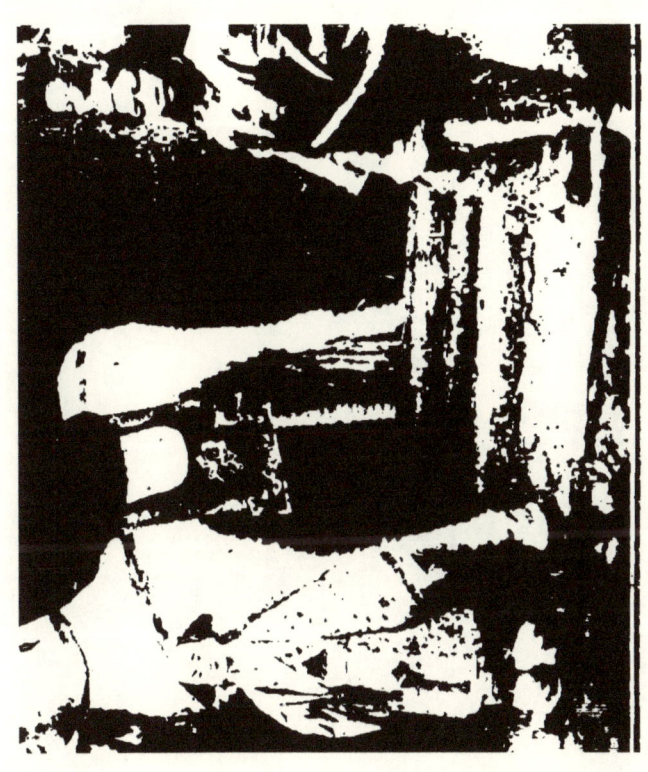

Gifts sent into the Spirit World.—*Page* 110.

is quite fresh in my memory—that it was here I spent a dreadful night: such a night as has often since made me brimful of thankfulness for even indifferent accommodation. It was here I suffered from the combined effects of the pungent straw smoke, the shrill-voiced landlady, and the yelping cur. But to-night, after trying several inns, where they would not receive us, we hammered—ay, and vigorously too—for admission at the door of that particular hotel in which I had suffered so many things. I heard the lady shouting at her henpecked husband, and I heard the cur joining with its yelp in the incessant din. Goodness knows if it had been going on all the time I had been away! We failed to get them to open the door of " The Everlasting Peaceful " (Oh the irony of fate!); and after no little difficulty we got into a shockingly dirty room in a small-sized inn. I must soon have forgotten my troubles in sleep. At length, I thought, however, that I had only slept a few moments when I was awakened by the screaming of the shrill-voiced landlady, and by the yelping cur feeding on my right heel. I woke up to consciousness to hear my servant gravely telling me that it was time to get up, and to feel a stinging pain in my heel. I had noticed the day before that at intervals a sharp pain shot through it. But at night when I drew off my long boots before lying down, I was so tired I did not look to see what my heel was like—I did not take off my socks. This morning, then, I found that my foot must have been bleeding yesterday, and that now my woollen sock was firmly sealed into the sore.

I was not able to walk, so I had to get into the shentzŭ before we started. It was barely five o'clock when we left Yao-kow. On account of the snow lying so deep we did not get on very quickly. About nine o'clock we passed through Chang-lo, a fairly substantial looking town. The county of the same name, and of which it is the capital, has some valuable hills in its southern part. In a splendid range lying on our right there were beautiful specimens of limestone, trap rock, and amagdeloid. Coal of a good quality is found cropping out here and there among the range.

At noon we rested at an inn in the northern suburb of Wei-hsien to let the animals be fed, and to change some silver.

Oh those money changers! Jewish ones were once whipped out of the Temple in Jerusalem; but compared with the general run of Chinese money-changers Shylock, the Jew, was the veriest open-handed, soft-hearted gentleman. Come with me to this changer's place of business, and see and hear how things are done.

Our servant, who has been making many inquiries

as we came along, and who knows the ways of the people with whom we are to deal, informs us before we enter into the presence of our Chinese Shylock, that silver of medium quality is changing for the day at fourteen hundred cash per liang, or tael, or ounce. As our former experience has taught us never to carry anything but the best silver, we enter the presence of the robber with our minds quite clear as to the value of every ounce of the precious metal we possess. Our weighing utensils and our silver are carefully kept out of sight as we enter.

After we have respectfully asked the hook-nosed, great-goggled scoundrel who is to swindle us, as to his honourable name, exalted age, and noble house, and been answered in a mild, deprecating, deferential air, we essay to bring forward the business we are there to transact. But the wily villain knows that time is precious to all foreigners, and he plies us politely with many, many questions, to refrain from answering which graciously would be most unbecoming on our part. At length we bring out our beautiful silver, and the hawk eyes cannot hide the gleam of pleasure at the sight, though the same stolid look sits on his unreadable face. He knows that he never has had purer metal in his hand, and yet he takes it up with an air of perfectly assumed indifference, looks at it as if a glance were all that was needed, and almost tosses it carelessly down on the counter without weighing it.

"Foreign gentlemen always deal in the first quality of silver," says my Shylock. "Some unprincipled person has imposed shamefully on the distinguished caller." That was not a bad opening for "the heathen Chinee." Just look at it. It is packed full of ability. In those few words he meant to impress me with, at least, the following facts: He knew the ways of foreign gentlemen; he knew good silver when he saw it; foreign gentlemen dealt with good silver; his present caller did not intend to impose upon the honest money-changer; the eminent foreigner had been cheated by some wicked person; he, the money-changer, was sorry for the illustrious traveller, and feared that he might not be able to do business with him, seeing that the silver was of so poor quality.

We lift our silver, smile, bring out our scales and weigh the piece with an air that tells our Shylock that we have been there before. He brings out his weights also, and tests our standard without a word. The look that he tries to gather on his face is one of sorrow—sorrow on our behalf, that we should have been so deceived by some bad man. The villain is afraid that he is not going to make as much out of the business as he had hoped. But there is no lack of cheat in this crafty Chinaman. We talk and talk.

Does he ridicule?—I am sarcastic. Is he modest and retiring?—I am bashfulness personified. But whether we are acrimonious or amiable, invidious or benign, we must follow out the recognised rules of the game, and ever be polite. We may just make up our minds to be cheated some, or we would be far better not to venture out on a journey. One is cheated about the quality of their silver, cheated about the weight of the piece, cheated about the rate of exchange, cheated a little even in the counting of the cash.

How to get more cash seems to be the problem that meets every Chinese who survives the days of childhood. Indeed, it is questionable if the problem is not instilled at the mother's breast; for is not her own thought daily and hourly turning around this very point. The struggle for bare existence is so severe in China, that cash—the symbol of everything eatable, drinkable, and wearable—monopolises a large share of the conversation among the hungry, the thirsty, and the naked. Wherever people are met, cash is almost invariably the subject of discourse. They talk cash. They think cash. They live cash. Some of the most amusing stories for children treat on the subject of cash: it is said that three-fifths of all the proverbs in the Chinese language have seen the light first through the small, square hole in the centre of a cash.

Well, after a wearisome time our business was completed, and our servant bundled the "filthy lucre" into the cash bag—the word qualifying the lucre here is used in a real as well as a figurative sense. Wang, this Chinese Shylock, is volubly protesting that he has been robbed, and at the same time he is warning us that we should change some more silver at his place, as he knows that we shall have great difficulty in doing business further east. But we cannot wait longer, so I part from him, giving him a kind of left-handed good-bye in the form of the brief proverb from the Confucian Analect: "Fu kuei tsai t'ien," meaning "Riches and honours depend upon heaven." To this he replied by using one of the terse sayings of the ancients: "Ih lu fuh hsing," "May a happy star light your way." After all, even though we had robbed him, he was surely a very kindly Shylock.

The animals had got a good feed by the time we got back to the inn, and as everything, strangely enough, was ready, we set out across the great plain which lies to the east and north-east of Wei-hsien. Owing to my lameness I had to sit in the shentzŭ all the way. It was no pleasant part of the journey. The wind was blowing fiercely across the plain: if the snow had not been too wet to drift, we would not have dared to travel. At times it seemed as if the shentzŭ would have been blown to pieces.

When our path lay for a little in such a direction as gave us the wind on our back, we were blown forward at such a rate that that rear mule, blind and lame as it was, fairly cantered before the gale. Before we arrived at our destination for the night, the snow had so far dried, that great white waves were rolling across the plain, and covering every evidence of a path. It was long after the usual time for travellers to arrive, when we gladly took refuge at the village inn at Wang-lu.

CHAPTER XII

It was bitterly cold when we set out from Wang-lu, a little after 5 A.M. The snow was hard enough and dry enough this morning. In many parts of the road it was drifted so badly, that we had more than once to make wide detours in order to get forward. But the mules seemed to know that they were drawing nearer home, and they kept to their work in earnest. Now and again they waded through drifts so deep, that the shentzŭ was actually dragged by the willing workers along the surface of the snow. The boatmen at the Huai-ho were much surprised to see a shentzŭ turn up on the west side of the river on such a morning, and at so early an hour.

Although the Huai-ho was frozen over, the ice could not be depended upon; so we had to make use of a flotilla, or pontoon of boats and barges, which the owners had anchored across the river. There was quite a number of men at hand—willing men, who picked the shentzŭ from the backs of our mules, and carried it along the unstable way at no small speed. I did not leave my seat, and therefore got the full benefit of the passage. It was somewhat rough. Now one of the boats would swing a little further out of line than usual, and would be brought up with such a painfully sharp jerk, when it bumped against the jagged edge of the ice, that more than one of the carriers were sure to collapse at the moment of impact. Again, some one of them would put his foot just at the place where a board should have been but was not, and then the traveller came through a sharp, if short, season of rolling and pitching. Here a poor fellow was on the ice; there another was in the bottom of one of the boats; a third, and he seemed to feel as if the gods had been unpropitious indeed, had slipped his foot into the ice-cold water. But they were all as happy as schoolboys just let loose.

Without any serious mishap we got to the other side, and then the men went back to bring the animals across. They had some rare amusement. "That rear mule" lay down in one of the boats. Now it so happened that one of the helpers stumbled into the same locality at the same time. What fun the other carriers got out of this! They shouted at the man who lay in the bottom of the boat to get up. In doing so, they used the phrase for telling one to get up out of bed. They yelled at him. They exhorted him. They warned the poor fellow who had fallen in beside that wicked, old, knowing, rear mule, that if he did not get up quickly his lady would kick him out. At length, however, the passage was accomplished, and we were hastening forward as speedily as possible.

About noon we crossed the long stone bridge over the Hsin-ho. It was almost 200 yards long, was very narrow, and had no parapet. The slabs were smooth, and the water-carriers, as they came and went with their loads, had carelessly spilt as much water on the smooth stones as had produced an actually glassy surface at the first breath of the north wind. We took a long time to get across. I must say that Pateo looked frightened on the bridge. When we were almost in the middle of the predicament a water-carrier yelled at Pateo to be careful; informing him that the day before a shentzŭ had been blown over into the river, and that that very forenoon a donkey and its rider had slipped over the edge. My driver really shook, and I did not feel comfortable—a prisoner, so to speak, shut up in that trap of a conveyance. "Last year," the garrulous one continued, "there was not so much wind as there is to-day, but there were five carts, seven shentzŭs"—— We heard no more, and were glad to be out of reach of the voice of the croaker.

After another half hour we rested at a place

called Hsin-ho-chieh. I had a very characteristic conversation with my innkeeper while resting there. Time seemed to be hanging heavy on his hands. So after I had eaten, and the men were preparing for a start, he came into my room. He was a thoroughly intelligent man, and was not too far away from the coast to know what was going on in the outside world.

"I invite you to sit," said I, rising.

"Sit, sit, I entreat you," he answered, as if grieved with me for attempting to lower myself by standing in his presence. At the same time he made a feint as if he would be seated.

After a little while we both sat down, the innkeeper making believe that I was his host, seeing that he was in my room, and I, addressing him as my host, seeing that I was in his house.

"Your honourable name, sir?" said he.

"How could I mention it before I had heard the name of my host?" replied I. "Your distinguished name, sir?"

"I am ashamed to mention it to my noble host; but my disreputable surname is Chang. May I hear the name of the great traveller?" was the reply.

"My mean cognomen is Tong," I answered.

"How many eat rice in the house of the illustrious foreign gentleman?" This, according to Chinese etiquette, was really an inquiry as to the number of sons I had in my family. When the traveller can say that even one eats rice in his house he is congratulated; but if he has no sons, and makes a hint to that effect in his answer, his interrogator with much ability turns the subject off.

Having dealt with families, ages, and other points, this innkeeper proceeded to prove both his curiosity and his intelligence.

"The great one's honourable country?" said he.

"What do you think now? See if you could guess it," I replied; as I wanted to break down a little of the formality, and get at what the man was thinking. He looked at me for a little time and then—

"Fa-kuoh?" he suggested hesitatingly.

"No, thank you, I am not French," I answered.

"Ah!" was all he said; but he looked pleased. The intelligent Chinese do not like the French. The Franco-Chinese affair at Foochow is still too fresh in their memories for any love to be lost between the two.

"Mei-kuoh?" he ventured, after again examining my features critically.

"Wrong again," I replied, laughing, "I am not an American."

Once more he gave expression to a prolonged

"Ah," which had in it something of pleasure and relief, I fancied. The Chinese have no love for Americans generally, on account of the exclusion bill passed a few years ago. This remark does not refer to American missionaries at all.

"I seem not to be able to mention the country my great host has honoured by his birth," said he; "may I ask the noble stranger to name it himself."

Now, all the time perhaps this knowing heathen had a pretty good idea that I was a Britisher. Certainly I would not have been in the least surprised to learn, that he had got almost all he wanted to know about me from Pateo, or from my servant before he came in to see me. Still, as I have already said, one must follow the rules of the game; hence question and answer *a la regle*.

Being brought to the point, then, as to my nationality, I replied—

"O shï Ing-kuoh:" "I am English." The Chinaman understands that to mean a Britisher: he does not descend to such fine distinctions as to know that a Scotsman at home does not feel flattered to be called an Englishman, and *vice versa*.

At once the man before me was on his feet. He put his hands together, one inside the other, and raised them to the level of his eyes. Then he made a most graceful salaam, bringing down his hands, still together, so far as to his knees. He raised himself to his full height, brought his hands up to the level of his eyes as before, and exclaimed—

"Ah, Great England! Honoured sir, I congratulate you." With well assumed humility—for I think that no country is worthy of being compared with Britain—I protest against such flattery, murmur something about my country being very small and away off the outskirts of the Great Middle Kingdom (China); but he will hear nothing from me on this point.

"Great England! Great England!" he kept rolling as a sweet morsel under his tongue—and the performance was over.

We tore ourselves away from the inn of "Imperishable Righteousness," and held forward into what was to me quite a new district. As we advanced we crossed and recrossed the line of telegraph. Believe me, the singing at the posts sounded very pleasant to one making for home. I should not forget to say, that at one point that afternoon our cavalcade got into a drove of donkeys. It was most amusing to see men and boys with baskets on their arms, and a little trident in their right hands, rushing from the snow-covered cottage, here and there, to follow in the rear of the drove and gather the uncertain droppings on the way.

When we arrived at Sha-ho we were all well tired.

This place had some of the most substantial-looking buildings I had seen on my journey. About thirty li to the north I had landed from the steamer *Kwang-chi* a year and a half previously, and had had a look at the straw-braid district of which Sha-ho was the headquarters. The place looked like a thorough business centre. That night I slept in the best Chinese inn I have ever seen. My room had a wooden floor, no less; and the walls were well papered with a good imitation of foreign wall-paper.

Next morning, Friday, we were up before three o'clock, as we hoped to reach the foreigners' houses at the city of Huang-hsien on Saturday night, and we had two long days' journey before us. It seemed very dark when we set out. Just before taking the road, I asked Pateo if he knew the way well. He looked quite indignant, and talked so long in reply to the simple question, that I began to be suspicious about him. He asserted and reasserted that he could easily go home from where he stood with his eyes shut. He banged things about, whacked the mules, and acted in such a way as almost convinced me that he really did not know the road. Well, we set out, but I had my mind made up to keep my eye on Pateo. After half-an-hour or so, and we seemed to be on a great flat stretch; I was sitting in the shentzŭ watching one of the pointers of Ursa Major.

But if we were going anything steadily, I concluded that never had star gyrated as that pointer was doing. At length the whole constellation mentioned got out of my range of vision past the side of the shentzŭ. In half-an-hour more or so I stopped Pateo and asked him in what direction we were going. At once he answered "East-north" —that was the direction in which we should have been going. I got him to bring his lantern, and on examining my pocket compass I found that we were hurrying on to the south-east. Possibly the Chinese that I used there and then was not very good—it came with such a rush. But I think it made an impression on that man.

I do not know that all muleteers are alike, but this man had a thorough aversion to ask any one to direct him. He went rushing on, evidently hoping to cover his ignorance, and hoping, too, that things would turn out all right in the end ; and the more he was advised, the more like his animals he became. To help him in his awkward position, Mr. Ü suggested to him that if he would let the mules alone they would find their way homeward, and the servant advised that Pateo should shut his eyes and go ahead—only he was to leave the lantern with the servant. Oh, but Pateo was a mad muleteer ! He whacked those mules, and he cursed those mules— particularly that rear mule. He railed at the lying compass that had exposed him, at the teacher for his unkind remark, and at the servant for daring, under such trying circumstances, to remind him of what had been said just before we had set out from the Sha-ho inn.

We were late of getting to our halting-place that forenoon. At Lai-chou-fu we rested at the western suburb, and partook of our mid-day meal. The teacher hurried into the city and bought for me a few very pretty ornaments in soapstone. He also bought a hundred very small idols and charms made of the same material, at *one cash each* (readers may have forgotten that a cash is equal to the twenty-fifth part of a penny). The hills in this district were full of soapstone and beautiful marble. Here the men work in the fields in the summer, and at quarrying and carving in the winter.

It was after six o'clock when we arrived at Chu-chiao, where we spent the night. Again we were fortunate in getting into a good inn, but the night was fearfully cold. In order to raise the temperature of my room I bought two ounces of Chinese wine and burned it. Before I set out on my journey I was advised by an experienced traveller to try that plan if at any time I got into a bitterly cold place. The result of burning a little wine was simply amazing. In a short time it raised the warmth of my room ten or fifteen degrees.

Next day we again set out at a very early hour, and after travelling a most trying road, and making a detour of five li to cross the Chieh-ho River, we reached Huang-shan-kuan, and rested there. The district through which we passed was well wooded, evident care being taken in the cultivation of the date tree.

Thirty li from our resting place we passed through White-Horse village, an important place holding a market every five days. There was a full market on when we arrived, and we had no little difficulty in getting through. The people seemed to be packed together on the space left in the main street, after the merchandise had been properly spread out. Such a variety of articles was there: pails and pitchforks, shoes and hats, ribbons and trinkets, cakes and sweets, pigs and poultry, beancurd and rice, vegetables and dried fruits, cloth and furs, snow-boots and sheepskin gowns, seeds for the coming spring, rakes and—refuse! People were well used with foreigners there: many of them scarcely turned their heads as I passed; everybody was bent on business.

The snow was gradually getting deeper as we journeyed, and before our day's travel was over we were going very slowly indeed. With thankful hearts we reached Huang-hsien, and soon found our way to the foreigners' houses, a little to the north of the city. I had a most delightful welcome from Mr. and Mrs. P——, of the American Southern Baptist Mission, at whose home I was entertained most hospitably.

The city of Huang-hsien is about sixty li from the capital of the fu, and stands on the great high road between Chefoo and Peking. It is a most substantially built town. The people are mostly well-off, and are said to be very difficult to deal with. From Huang-hsien, which is the centre of the trade, enormous quantities of vermicelli are exported.

In 1885, after long trouble and waiting, the American Southern Baptist Mission had first secured a house in this city. But the station had been occupied only a short time by Messrs. D—— and J——, when the former died of consumption, and the latter returned to America in broken health. Then in 1888 Mr. and Mrs. P——, accompanied by the wife of the missionary who had died here, re-opened this station, where the house had never been given up. Before the end of that same year, however, Mrs. D—— was forced, on account of failing health, to return to the United States. Huang-hsien was reinforced in 1889 by Mr. and Mrs. L——, who were working there at the time of my visit, and whose fellowship I much enjoyed during the quiet Sabbath I spent in the compound. Every little mission station in China has its touching history. It has often occurred to me that it would be no mean or unprofitable task to undertake, to collect and issue a brief series of such histories in the interest of the world-wide mission cause.

CHAPTER XIII

AFTER such a calm and peaceful Sabbath as we had spent at Huang-hsien, we would have been able to start at an early hour this morning had it been possible to have got the city gate opened by fair means. It would have been necessary to have bribed the gate-keeper, and that I was unwilling to do—though a very small bribe would have sufficed. We did not leave the city till seven o'clock.

For the first forty li we had what I might call a good road; after that we got in among the hills, and many an awkward fix we found ourselves in. It was just as well that the mules had had a good day's rest at Huang-hsien; they needed all the strength they had to-day. And although I am not "an apologist for the mule," and certainly not for "that rear mule," which by this time the reader has commenced to know about, I must say that they kept at their hard work steadily. The roads were so bad that travellers were few; I do not think we saw more than half-a-dozen during the whole of that forenoon. Our cavalcade was in good spirits, however, for every step was taking us so much nearer home. If we managed to keep up the speed we had been doing, this would be our last night in the inns.

About eighteen li from Huang-hsien we crossed the Ta-ho. We had got only ten li in among the hills when we rested at Tse-kow-t'ien. There we had an explanation of the small number of people on the way. The courtyard was full of beasts of burden, carts, shentzŭs, and barrows; almost all the smaller rooms of the inn had their full complement of men, not to mention merchandise. The large general room had the look of a wholesale variety store. Some of the men were busy gambling; others, at different stages of the opium stupor, were lying in the out of the way small rooms; while not a few were lounging about among the stuff. One could not but marvel at the variety, as well as the quantity, of the goods that one saw in such a small space—bales of cloth, boxes of oil, matches and incense sticks by the million, vermicelli, straw-braid, paper, and furs.

On our arrival, the travellers who were wishing to go west were very particular in their inquiries as to the road—the depth of snow, the thickness of ice, and the general probabilities of their being able to get through. We gave them what information we could; but as it was snowing heavily at the time we reached the inn of "Imperishable Fragrance," at Tse-kow-t'ien, nobody attempted to set out.

After we had got our outer man thawed, and our inner man refreshed, we decided, sorely against our will, that we should not set out in the face of such a snowstorm as was impending. Had the roads been clear to begin with, we would have gone forward in spite of the threatening storm; but there were several in the inn who had already waited two or three days on account of uncertainty of weather and the depth of snow on the road to Chefoo. Having reluctantly decided to remain in the "Imperishable Fragrance," I made myself as friendly as I could with the other travellers.

As can well be understood, time was hanging heavy on some of those who had been waiting for days. But there was an entire absence of that moustache-chewing, heel-kicking impatience that marks the average Britisher after a two hours' detention on a journey. I could draw from the conversation of my philosophic fellow-travellers that they had been making the time pass as pleasantly as possible. Although they had not been long together—speaking from the Chinese point of view—they seemed to have picked out each other's peculiarities and little failings. One man had gained for himself the sobriquet of "Nine-bowls," on account of the number of basins of rice that he could hide at one sitting. Another was called "Wisdom"—he was the fool of the company. One was designated "Wine-jar;" and another was honoured with the name "Chih-ku-sï," which means literally "Know-ancient-matters"—he was a famous teller of stories.

I had been, I must again confess, most unwilling to put off time at that inn, in spite of its euphonious name; but, before an hour was over, I was really thankful that I had been delayed. In making myself so free with my fellow-travellers, they acted quite naturally before me, and I had an opportunity of learning something of their ways that I had never thought of, nor had I ever seen it mentioned in any work relating to China or to the Chinese.

Upwards of a dozen men were sitting about on packages and stools fairly close together, when one asked another to "relate some ancient matter." The one invited to speak had plenty in his repertoire, I had no doubt—every Chinaman's mind is a perfect storehouse of "ancient matters"—but he modestly declined, proposing at the same time that Chih-ku-sï should hold forth to them.

"The man who knew the ancients" was ready,

but said, "How can I begin unless some one pull out my drawer? My drawer is shut."

There was a little hesitation on the part of those sitting about. Quite a number of others, who seemed to have intuitively guessed that a story was to be told, drew close up to the Chih-ku-sï.

"Some of you begin with a short story," said he. "It may pull out my drawer, and I may be able to bring out something I shall be pleased to tell and you to hear."

Again there was a little silence, and a few more quietly sat down among the expectant hearers. The speaker, looking round about him as if perplexed that his memory should have proved so fickle, murmured as if half to himself, "Now, where—where shall I begin? Will nobody pull out my drawer?"

Then one man, willing to oblige, tried to stir up the memory of the story-teller:

"A week ago to-day," said he, "as I was going along the road I saw a man. He was short, and he was fat. His eyes were the eyes of a wolf, his hair was the hair of age, his step was the step of a child."

All eyes were turned to the story-teller to note what effect the suggestion was making upon him; but Chih-ku-sï was silent. Nothing that had been said had as yet touched a cord in his memory. Then another man ventured:

"On the third of the present moon, a bitterly cold day, I saw a father and his two sons going to market. The younger son was comfortably dressed, and sitting in the barrow. The other son was poorly clad, and very thin. 'Yes!' I said to myself, 'the younger son is the son of the present wife, but——'"

"Ah, ya!" exclaimed Chih-ku-sï, "you have me now. My drawer is out, and it is full of such."

There is a little rustling and coughing as they settle down to listen, the story-teller himself taking some time to get his throat cleared, and evidently going through some of the premonitory symptoms of sea sickness in the process. But now he is ready.

"The story that I am going to relate to you," said he, "is entitled 'Pien-ta-lu-wha'—'Beat with the Whip, and the Rush Flowers fly.'"

Here there was just the last opportunity given for coughing, and "the man who knew the ancients" set out under full sail:

"Confucius had a disciple called Ming-tzŭ-k'ien. This disciple was noted for the reverence he paid to his parents. No doubt he had a good mother; but he, too, was a good son. Good sons make glad fathers and mothers. The great teacher often spoke with pleasure of his willing and obedient pupil.

"When Ming-tzŭ-k'ien was twelve years of age his mother died. Soon he had a stepmother. By-and-by his stepmother had two sons, to whom she gave all her love and care, and whom she treated well; but she treated Ming-tzŭ-k'ien most shamefully.

"The father did not notice the bad treatment that his first-born was daily made to undergo. Outwardly the mother seemed to treat all the children alike. Ming-tzŭ-k'ien was exceedingly unwilling to tell his father about it, for he feared that his father would be so angry that there would be strife in the home. He feared that the stepmother might be beaten or even sold, and that little King-Üin, the Propitious Cloud, and Fuh-Li, the Possessor of Rectitude, whom he had learned to love, would die of grief. King-Üin and Fuh-Li were his half-brothers. So he waited on patiently.

"Once in the winter time, however, his father went out on a short journey. He called Ming-tzŭ-k'ien, King-Üin, and Fuh-Li to pull his cart. They set out. The father sat in the cart, and the three sons pulled. It was bitterly, bitterly cold. Ming-tzŭ-k'ien was shivering all the time, but his brothers looked quite warm. The father, observing that his eldest son's clothes were thickly wadded, while those of the two younger were but thinly done, and that for all that Ming-tzŭ-k'ien shivered with cold, while King Üin and Fuh-Li were very hot, was very angry. He thought that his eldest boy was lazy, and of no use. At last the father got so angry that when Ming-tzŭ-k'ien trembled and shivered so much that the rope by which he was pulling dropped from his numbed fingers, his father used the whip on him again and again.

"By-and-by Ming-tsŭ-k'ien's clothes were torn and ragged with the whipping. But what was this! What was this! Out from the rent garment flew the flowers of the hollow-stemmed reed.

"Now the father understood. Well he knew, and well his wife knew, that there was no heat in this kind of wadding. He was much surprised to see that it had been used in his eldest son's clothing. Down from his cart he came and examined the clothes of the younger boys. Quickly he tore a small piece open. And what did he find? The flowers of the hollow-stemmed reeds? No, no. Were the clothes wadded with cotton even? Oh no; nothing so poor as cotton—though that is looked upon as very good—for the sons of the second wife. It was silk, very expensive floss silk, with which their garments were nicely wadded.

"The father wept in great bitterness. He now understood something of what his eldest son must have been enduring in silence for the sake of peace. He gave up the intended journey, and with a determined look on his face turned towards home. At once on his arrival he rebuked and reproved his wife sternly. He ordered her to leave his house, never to return. In olden times that custom held as law in China.

"Ming-tzŭ-k'ien, seeing what was about to take place, went and pled with his father. But in those days long, long ago boys were respectful. They did not use many words when speaking with their fathers. Let the young men here take note. So he only said, 'Mother here, one son cold: mother away, cold would be three.' 'What do you mean by that, my son?' queried the father. The lad thus getting permission to enlarge, answered, 'Now I am the only stepson: I alone am cold. But if this mother go away, another will decidedly come. Then three of us shall have a stepmother: three of us shall be cold.'

"'Right, my boy,' said the father thoughtfully; 'your present mother shall stay.' And she did. When she learned what Ming-tzŭ-k'ien had done for her, she repented with tears, and loved him ever after as her own son. Never again did he shiver with cold: never again was he beaten with the whip till the rush flowers flew.

"From this it may be seen that Ming-tzŭ-k'ien not only reverenced his parents, but that he loved his brothers. He showed the fruit of the wisdom that comes from studying the great sage."

. . . .

What I have written does not do justice to the

story-teller nor to the finer points in the Chinese idiom. Still, it will give readers an idea of some of the lines of thought of this strange people.

As soon as that story was finished, one of the travellers, with whom I had had a little friendly chat before it began, said to me very deferentially, but loudly enough for several to hear: "Has the foreign gentleman any ancient matter he would relate to us? We would feel greatly honoured."

I politely protested that my Chinese words were so few that I was sure to run short before I had got properly commenced. I held back a little, just to add to their desire to hear, and to draw undivided attention to what I might say. Before beginning I said to my teacher, in a voice that all could hear—

"My teacher, Mr. Ü, will put me right if I use a wrong word, and help me if I get into a real difficulty. But you must all understand that I am only a beginner in the study of your great language."

"The title of my story," I began, "is 'The Noble Middleman.'"

At this stage, as before, the little rustling was repeated. There was some more coughing to be done, and the large general room was now packed, as the rest of the men had heard that the foreigner was going to relate "an ancient matter." I had a most attentive audience, as I told them the matchless story of the wondrous life of the Saviour. As nearly as I could I put it into Chinese dress, and kept it in the allegorical form. As I went on my audience drew closer as I spoke lower. All were bent towards me. Some on the outside of the circle were craning their necks and straining their ears. All were very still. They had never heard such a story. But I need not tell my readers what I said: it was just the old, old story of Jesus and His love.

I intended to have finished with this chapter. But whether it is that I am loth to leave my readers, whether it is that I feel free to prolong the trial of remaining away from home when I could by making a special effort reach it, or whether there is something in me as a chronicler that corresponds with what is in the cat when it toys with its prey before despatching it, I do not know. I feel, however, that I would require to stop too curtly if I had to pull up in a few lines here. "Under the circumstances"—happy phrase covering the failures and foibles of men!—readers will, perhaps, bear with me for giving one brief chapter in conclusion.

CHAPTER XIV

WHEN I had finished my story many of the men seemed deeply impressed; and they gave the best proof they could have given of this—there was no further call for "ancient matter."

By this time the snow had ceased to fall, and as the afternoon was clearing up we ventured out once more. But we had a rough-and-tumble experience all the way. At one place a cart ran into the shentzŭ and almost capsized us. Fortunately a high bank of snow was just at the right place. At another point both mules fell, but they got up again without my getting out. Still we kept at it.

That night when we arrived at "The Beacon Comfort" inn at Wo-lo-tzŭ, about nine o'clock, we had hard work to get the people to open the door. They seemed to have been asleep for hours, and would scarcely take it in that we were not robbers. Of course, our arrival caused a great stir. The most disconcerting part of the noise to me was the statement that we had really the roughest part of the road to get over on the coming day, that

is, if we should be able to travel. After a good
night's rest we got up at 5.30 on the morning of
the 20th January, and were very soon on the way,
hoping to reach Chefoo that evening. Immediately
after setting out we had a most difficult hill to
ascend and descend. We got over it, however,
without any mishap. I was told that this was
the only really difficult hill that we would have
before reaching Yen-t'ai (Chefoo), and I began to
be hopeful. Vain hope! there was range after
range—at least, they looked like mountain ranges
to one with a lame foot cooped up in a shentzŭ.
As early in the day as 9.20 I got a glimpse of
the fort to the west of Chefoo, and was delighted to
see it. Now and again as we got on the high ground
we were catching glimpses of the sea.

At ten o'clock we passed the village of Ku-hsien.
It was at this place that Messrs. Holmes and Parker
were murdered by a band of marauders in 1861. It
is a tragic and gruesome story.

During the autumn of the year mentioned almost
the whole eastern part of the province of Shantung
was ravaged and pillaged by a band of rebels. The
people in every district met with the most inhuman
treatment. Messrs. Parker of Chu-ki and A. L.
Holmes of Yen-t'ai, hoping to be able to prevail
upon the leaders to withhold their men from such
awful cruelties as were being practised, went out

on their mission of mercy on the 7th of October. They met with the destroyers near the village of Ku-hsien, about thirty miles west-south-west from Chefoo. Without the slightest compunction the murderous band rushed upon them and stabbed them to death, without giving the bearers of the flag of peace the least opportunity of saying why they had come. Immediately afterwards the band decamped, fearing, perhaps, the result of their dastardly murder of the foreigners.

Although the marauders made it a practice to leave no survivors in any village they attacked, they judiciously left a number alive in Ku-hsien, and possibly hoped that upon those survivors the guilt attaching to the murder of the foreign missionaries might fall. Alas, alas! the tender mercies of the wicked are cruel. The surviving villagers, after collecting a large quantity of millet stalks, took the two sadly-disfigured bodies of their would-be deliverers, placed them on the stalks collected, and set fire to the whole. They hoped to consume the bodies to ashes, and thus hide any possible connection that their village might have had with the death of the foreigners. Some of the millet stalks were damp, however, and the object was not accomplished.

That was a terrible blow to the work of the Mission. Yet a more terrible one would, in all probability, have been received if the other members of it, along with Mrs. Holmes, had not had a marvellous escape from Chu-ki very soon after.

One midnight, while the weary watchers waited for the sound of their loved ones' footsteps, which, alas! they were to hear no more, a hurried message came from the British Consul at Chefoo. He had sent horses for them, and the foreigners were to make for Yen-t'ai with all speed, as the rebels were almost upon them. Quickly they were on the way. They had left none too soon. Scarcely had they got clear of the village when it was entered by a fierce band of the marauders. The house that had just been evacuated by the foreign ladies and their children was immediately attacked; everything of value was either destroyed or carried away, and the house itself left a blackened ruin.

By-and-by a search party from Chefoo arrived at Ku-hsien. After long and diligent search they discovered the mutilated and scorched remains of the two murdered missionaries. They carried them away to the port, and afterwards took them out to a little island near to the lighthouse. There they buried them—mutilated, disfigured, scorched, putrifying—to be raised one day divinely fair.

Before leaving this subject, I feel that I ought to say a word in vindication of what must seem to some readers a recklessness on the part of the two murdered men.

Some months previously, Mr. Holmes had met with a larger number of the T'ai Ping rebels in the south, and had been very well treated by them. When it was noised abroad in Shantung province that a band of rebels had come from the south, and that they were committing shocking barbarities upon helpless women and children, Mr. Holmes, concluding that it was part of the same band that he had met before, at once determined to meet the leaders, and try, if possible, to induce them to restrain their men from the wanton destruction of life and property. Mr. Parker would not think of allowing Mr. Holmes to go alone. They set out together, and met their fate in the village of Ku-hsien, as described above.

. . . . . .

About eleven o'clock we rested at Kang-yü. At this place the Têng-chou-fu and Huang-hsien roads unite. Close by there are some most interesting mounds. These mark the graves of kings who reigned over a small but powerful kingdom, whose capital was built in the plain to the north-east of Kang-yü, and which had an extensive trade with Corea and Japan. This kingdom, we read, was not subject to China, but existed in defiance of it.

THE TOMB OF CONFUCIUS

Part of the old city wall of the capital can be seen from the road.

But I must confess I did not care much either for city walls or capitals that snowy day. The fort to the west of Yen-ta'i seemed to come no nearer, but still we held on. On reaching the village of Chu-k'i, we found that the roads were turning worse. As we went up the hill at the fort, I counted seven mules all down at one time —the road was so slippery. We had a breakdown to the east of Tong-hsin, but did not mind it much, as we were almost in sight of home. Very soon I was at my own fireside, and found all well.

I had been away only thirty-six days, and had travelled scarcely a thousand miles, but yet I was exceedingly thankful to get into my haven. It was with a heart full of the deepest gratitude to my Heavenly Father, who had taken such care over me, that I found myself once again at The Collegiate School, Chefoo.

Printed by BALLANTYNE, HANSON & CO.
Edinburgh and London

Books for Young Readers.

LIST OF SOME NEW PUBLICATIONS.

By the Rev. J. R. MILLER, D.D.

GLIMPSES THROUGH LIFE'S WINDOW. Selections from the writings of the Rev. J. R. MILLER, D.D., Author of "Making the Most of Life." Small Crown 8vo, with Portrait. Gilt top, 2s. 6d.

GIRLS; FAULTS AND IDEALS. With Quotations from Girls' Letters. By the Rev. J. R. MILLER, D.D. Crown 8vo. 6d.

YOUNG MEN; FAULTS AND IDEALS. With Quotations from Young Men's Letters. By the Rev. J. R. MILLER, D.D. Crown 8vo. 6d.

By DEAN FARRAR, &c. &c.

BIBLICAL CHARACTER SKETCHES. By DEAN FARRAR, &c. &c. Crown 8vo. 3s. 6d.

By F. A. ATKINS.

ASPIRATION AND ACHIEVEMENT. A Book for Young Men. By F. A. Atkins, Author of "Moral Muscle," &c. &c., and Editor of the "Young Man." Cloth. Small Crown 8vo. 1s.

By ALEX. ARMSTRONG, F.R.G.S.

IN A MULE LITTER TO THE TOMB OF CONFUCIUS. By ALEX. ARMSTRONG, F.R.G.S. Crown 8vo. Profusely Illustrated. 2s. 6d.

By the Rev. S. F. HARRIS.

EARNEST YOUNG HEROES. Ion Keith Falconer, Hedley Vicars, Lieutenant Boldero, R.N., and Mackay of Uganda. By the Rev. F. S. HARRIS. With Portraits. Crown 8vo. 2s.

By EMILY DIBDIN.

SOME COMMON INSECTS. By EMILY DIBDIN, Author of "Spoilt Twins." Profusely Illustrated. Crown 8vo. 1s. 6d. Golden Silence Series.

By the Rev. F. BOURDILLON.

THE PRODIGAL AT HOME AGAIN. By the Rev. F. BOURDILLON, M.A., Author of "Alone with God," "A Help to Family Worship," &c. &c. Ex. Pott 8vo. 1s. cloth; 2s. roan.

By the Rev. E. J. HARDY.

IN THE FOOTPRINTS OF ST. PAUL. By the Rev. E. J. HARDY, Author of "How to be Happy though Married," "Uncle John's Talks with His Nephews," &c. With Map and Illustrations. Small Crown 8vo. 2s. 6d.

James Nisbet & Co.'s List.

THE "BERNERS" SERIES.

With numerous Illustrations. Handsomely bound in cloth, with bevelled boards and gilt edges. Extra crown 8vo. Price 5s. each.

5s. each.
1. THE WALRUS HUNTERS. A Tale of Esquimaux Land. By R. M. Ballantyne.
2. THE CLOSE OF ST. CHRISTOPHER'S. By Mrs. Marshall.
3. NEW RELATIONS. A Story for Girls. By Mrs. Marshall.
4. THOSE THREE; or, Little Wings. A Story for Girls. By Mrs. Marshall.
5. LAUREL CROWNS; or, Griselda's Aim. By Mrs. Marshall.
6. HOUSES ON WHEELS. A Story for Children. By Mrs. Marshall.
7. STRANGE YET TRUE. By Dr. Macaulay.
8. THE DUKE'S PAGE; or, In the Days of Luther. By Sarah M. S. Clarke.
9. BARON AND SQUIRE. A Story of the Thirty Years' War. By Sarah M. S. Clarke.
10. STEADY YOUR HELM. By W. C. Metcalfe.
11. ABOVE BOARD: A Tale of Adventure on the Sea. By W. C. Metcalfe.
12. LIZETTE AND HER MISSION. By Mrs. Marshall.
13. FROM PLOUGHSHARE TO PULPIT. By Gordon Stables, M.D., R.N.

Just Published.

14. THE LADY'S MANOR. By Mrs. Marshall. Illustrations by W. Lance.
15. THE CRUISE OF THE ROVER CARAVAN. By Gordon Stables, M.D., R.N. Illustrations by C. Whymper.
16. KATHERINE'S KEYS. By Sarah Doudney. Illustrations by Chas. Richardson.
17. TUDOR QUEENS AND PRINCESSES. By Sarah Tytler. With Portraits.
18. THE KING'S RECRUITS. By Sarah M. S. Clarke.

THE "CHIMES" SERIES.

Crown 8vo. Numerous Illustrations. 3s. 6d. each.
By Mrs. MARSHALL.

3s. 6d. each.
1. SILVER CHIMES; or, Olive.
2. DAPHNE'S DECISION; or, Which Shall it Be.
3. CASSANDRA'S CASKET.
4. POPPIES AND PANSIES.
5. REX AND REGINA; or, The Song of the River.
6. STORIES OF THE CATHEDRAL CITIES OF ENGLAND.
7. DEWDROPS AND DIAMONDS.
8. HEATHER AND HAREBELL.
9. THE ROSES OF RINGWOOD. A Story for Children.
10. IN THE PURPLE.
11. EASTWARD HO!

Books for Young Readers.

NEW FIVE SHILLING SERIES.

Demy 8vo, gilt edges. 5s. each.

THE DAYS OF BRUCE. By GRACE AGUILAR.

BARRIERS BURNED AWAY. By Rev. E. P. ROE.

THE "SWEETBRIAR" SERIES.

A New Series of Volumes. With Illustrations. Extra crown 8vo. 3s. 6d. each.

WORK, WAIT, WIN. By RUTH LAMB.   **3s. 6d. each.**

THE ANDERSONS. By Miss GIBERNE, Author of "The Dalrymples," &c.

SWEETBRIAR; or, Doings in Priorsthorpe Magna. By AGNES GIBERNE.

COULYING CASTLE; or, A Knight of the Olden Days. By AGNES GIBERNE.

AIMÉE: A Tale of the Days of James the Second. By AGNES GIBERNE.

LILLA THORNE'S VOYAGE; or, "That Far Remembrancer." By GRACE STEBBING.

NESTLETON MAGNA. By the Rev. JACKSON WRAY.

MATTHEW MELLOWDEW. By the Rev. JACKSON WRAY.

BETWIXT TWO FIRES. By the Rev. JACKSON WRAY.

SHIP DAPHNE. By the Rev. T. S. MILLINGTON. *Just Published.*

THE "ROUNDABOUT" SERIES.

Extra crown 8vo. 3s. 6d. each.

THE RIGHT ROAD. A Manual for Parents and Teachers. By J. KRAMER.   **3s. 6d. each.**

THROUGH BIBLE LANDS. Notes of Travel in Egypt, the Desert, and Palestine. Profusely Illustrated. By PHILIP SCHAFF, D.D., and an Essay on Egyptology and the Bible, by EDOUARD NAVILLE.

PALESTINE EXPLORED. By Rev. JAMES NEIL, M.A., late Incumbent of Christ Church, Jerusalem.

James Nisbet & Co.'s List.

THE "GOLDEN LADDER" SERIES.

*With Illustrations. Handsomely bound in cloth, gilt edges.
Crown 8vo. 3s. 6d. each.*

"Children welcome with glee the volumes comprised in Nisbet's 'Golden Ladder Series,' for they are full of interest, even though they are stories with a moral, which is always a high-toned one."—*Liverpool Courier.*

"'The Golden Ladder Series' of story-books, so much appreciated for their excellence. They can be all safely recommended to the notice of teachers as being especially suitable as rewards, while no school library can be said to be complete without a selection from them."—*Schoolmaster.*

3s. 6d. each.

THE GOLDEN LADDER: Stories Illustrative of the Beatitudes. By SUSAN and ANNA B. WARNER.
THE WIDE, WIDE WORLD. By SUSAN WARNER.
QUEECHY. By SUSAN WARNER.
MELBOURNE HOUSE. By SUSAN WARNER.
DAISY. By SUSAN WARNER.
DAISY IN THE FIELD. By SUSAN WARNER.
THE OLD HELMET. By SUSAN WARNER.
NETTIE'S MISSION: Stories Illustrative of the Lord's Prayer. By JULIA MATHEWS.
GLEN LUNA; or, Dollars and Cents. By ANNA B. WARNER.
DRAYTON HALL. Stories Illustrative of the Beatitudes. By JULIA MATHEWS.
WITHIN AND WITHOUT: A New England Story.
VINEGAR HILL STORIES. Illustrative of the Parable of the Sower. By ANNA B. WARNER.
LITTLE SUNBEAMS. By JOANNA MATHEWS.
WHAT SHE COULD AND OPPORTUNITIES. By SUSAN WARNER.
TRADING AND THE HOUSE IN TOWN.
DARE TO DO RIGHT. By JULIA MATHEWS.
HOLDEN WITH THE CORDS. By the Author of "Within and Without."
GIVING HONOUR: Containing "The Little Camp on Eagle Hill," and "Willow Brook." By SUSAN WARNER.
GIVING SERVICE: Containing "Sceptres and Crowns," and "The Flag of Truce." By SUSAN WARNER.
GIVING TRUST: Containing "Bread and Oranges," and "The Rapids of Niagara." By SUSAN WARNER.

** *The Tales in the last three Volumes are Illustrative of the* LORD'S PRAYER.

WYCH HAZEL. A Tale. By SUSAN and ANNA WARNER.
THE GOLD OF CHICKAREE. A Sequel to "Wych Hazel." By SUSAN and ANNA B. WARNER.
DIANA. By SUSAN WARNER.
MY DESIRE. By SUSAN WARNER.
THE END OF A COIL. By SUSAN WARNER.
THE LETTER OF CREDIT. By SUSAN WARNER.
NOBODY. By SUSAN WARNER.
STEPHEN, M.D. By SUSAN WARNER.
A RED WALLFLOWER. By SUSAN WARNER.
DAISY PLAINS. By SUSAN WARNER.
CROSS CORNERS. By ANNA B. WARNER.
MISTRESS MATCHETT'S MISTAKE. By EMMA MARSHALL.
YOURS AND MINE. By ANNA B. WARNER.
ONE LITTLE VEIN OF DROSS. By Mrs. RUTH LAMB.
OAK BEND; or, Patience and Her Schooling. By ANNA B. WARNER.
A CANDLE IN THE SEA; or, Winter at Seal's Head. A Book about Lighthouses. By Rev. E. A. RAND.
THE MILL ON SANDY CREEK. By Rev. E. A. RAND.
A SALT WATER HERO. By Rev. E. A. RAND.

www.ingramcontent.com/pod-product-compliance
Lightning Source LLC
Chambersburg PA
CBHW031446160426
43195CB00010BB/874